Lazy day
Brunches

Lazy day Brunches

Relaxed recipes for the morning

RYLAND PETERS & SMALL
LONDON • NEW YORK

Senior Designer Toni Kay
Editor Gillian Haslam
Head of Production
  Patricia Harrington
Art Director Leslie Harrington
Editorial Director Julia Charles
Publisher Cindy Richards
Indexer Vanessa Bird

First published in 2021 by
Ryland Peters & Small
20–21 Jockey's Fields, London
WC1R 4BW
and
341 E 116th St, New York NY 10029
www.rylandpeters.com

10 9 8 7 6 5 4 3 2 1

Recipe collection compiled
by Julia Charles

Text copyright © Caroline Artiss,
Ursula Ferrigno, Liz Franklin, Tonia
George, Carol Hilker, Kathy Kordalis,
Jenny Linford, Rosa Rigby, Laura
Santtini, Janet Sawyer, Jenny
Tschiesche 2021

Design and photographs copyright
© Ryland Peters & Small 2021

ISBN: 978-1-78879-284-4

Printed in China

A CIP record for this book is available
from the British Library.
US Library of Congress Cataloging-in-
Publication Data has been applied for.

Notes:
• Both British (Metric) and American
(Imperial plus US cups) are included
in these recipes for your convenience,
however it is important to work with
one set of measurements and not
alternate between the two within
a recipe.
• All spoon measurements are
level unless otherwise specified.
• All eggs are medium (UK) or large
(US), unless specified as large, in
which case US extra-large should be
used. Uncooked or partially cooked
eggs should not be served to
the very old, frail, young children,
pregnant women or those with
compromised immune systems.
• Ovens should be preheated
to the specified temperatures.
We recommend using an oven
thermometer. If using a fan-assisted
oven, adjust temperatures according
to the manufacturer's instructions.
• Whenever butter is called for within
these recipes, unsalted butter should
be used.
• When a recipe calls for the grated
zest of citrus fruit, buy unwaxed fruit
and wash well before using. If you
can only find treated fruit, scrub well
in warm soapy water before using.
• To sterilize preserving jars, wash
them in hot, soapy water and rinse
in boiling water. Place in a large
saucepan and cover with hot water.
With the saucepan lid on, bring the
water to a boil and continue boiling
for 15 minutes. Turn off the heat
and leave the jars in the hot water
until just before they are to be filled.
Invert the jars onto a clean dish
towel to dry. Sterilize the lids for
5 minutes, by boiling or according
to the manufacturer's instructions.
Jars should be filled and sealed
while they are still hot.

Contents

Introduction

For many, breakfast is the best and most important meal of the day, and on the weekends when the pace of life slows, there's nothing better than an indulgent brunch. With over 65 appetizing and modern recipes, this book offers dishes to suit everyone's brunchy style. From lazy lie-in treats and easy morning bites, to bountiful sharer plates and other wholesome offerings, here you'll find an array of yummy dishes to ensure your weekend mornings are both delicious and relaxed.

The tradition of 'brunch' – the playful combination of breakfast and lunch – is widely acknowledged to have its origin in Britain, where a plea was made for the typically heavy and onerous Sunday dinner to be replaced with something lighter in the late morning. Its popularity spread, reaching American hotels in the 1920s, specifically in Chicago, where the celebrity and elite sought a sophisticated late-morning meal in between their transcontinental rail journeys. By the 1930s, restaurants across the country caught onto the trend and began to offer similarly desirable brunch-specific menus, and even morning cocktails, for those wishing to use their Sundays to relax and catch up with friends. Since then, it's fair to say that the brunch phenomenon has soared and firmly taken its place as the king of weekend meals, playing host to all kinds of gatherings, from the eventful to the very casual, and everything in between. So whether you are cooking up a spontaneous treat for yourself, creating a cosy brunch for two, feeding the whole family or planning a delicious feast for a crowd, here you will find dishes for all occasions.

To kickstart your brunch, try one of the granola or porridge dishes. If you are in the mood for pancakes or waffles, you could opt for a classic maple and bacon combination or some French toast, or pull out all the stops and create cherry and ricotta blintzes served with a sour cherry soup. If eggs are your go-to brunch ingredient, try baked mushroom and egg ramekins, a frittata or breakfast tart or one of the new twists on the classic eggs Benedict. For summertime brunches, choose one of the tasty salads such as tomato and smoked mackerel or whip up a batch of sweet potato, pea and mint fritters.

To satisfy a sweet tooth, head to the pastries and breakfast bakes chapter, where you'll find such tempting treats as butterscotch-bacon brittle cinnamon rolls or spelt, banana and chocolate muffins. Try your hand at making your own preserves – there are great recipes for grape jelly, lemon curd and tomato vanilla jam, as well as chutneys to accompany your savoury dishes. And on the side, serve up a pomegranate and mint green tea or a blueberry coffee, or indulge yourself with a decadent pickle-back Martini.

With more than 65 appetizing and modern recipes, starting the day the right way has never been easier, or tastier!

Fruit, Grains & Oats

Blueberry & blackberry açai bowls

Overnight seed pots

Grainy porridge

Spiced sweet potato porridge

Quinoa granola with tropical fruit & coconut yogurt

Honey & vanilla granola

Super berry granola

Baked oat milk porridge with pears, almonds & date syrup

Melon & raspberry salad in stem ginger syrup

Orange-baked rhubarb

Roasted apricots with goat's curd puddles & oat clusters

Blueberry & blackberry açai bowls

200 ml/scant 1 cup
   coconut water
2 ripe bananas
100 g/½ cup frozen blueberries
50 g/¼ cup frozen blackberries
1 tablespoon açai powder
1 tablespoon rolled/old-
   fashioned oats (optional)

To Serve
100 g/¾ cup blueberries
50 g/⅓ cup blackberries
1 dragon fruit, sliced
50 g/⅓ cup kiwiberries
   or 1 whole kiwi, sliced
1 tablespoon flaked/slivered
   pistachios
a few sprigs of mint

Serves 4

As a food, açai pulp from the tribal Amazon belt is often blended with the starchy root vegetable manioc, and eaten as porridge. The taste is often described as reminiscent of wild berries and chocolate. The addition of its powdered form in a smoothie and blended with frozen berries gives you a great start to the day.

Blend the coconut water, bananas, frozen berries, açai powder and oats (if using) together in a blender until smooth. Stand for a few minutes to thicken.

Spoon into 4 small serving bowls. Arrange the fresh fruit, pistachios and mint on top and serve.

Overnight seed pots

Overnight pots are great for when you want breakfast ready to eat as soon as you get up. And even better — soaking nuts and seeds helps to de-activate enzyme inhibitors. These substances are naturally present in nuts and seeds, which protect them from digestion in the stomach. You can double, triple or quadruple the quantities of ingredients here if you want to prepare more than one serving.

Mixed seed pot

10 g/1 heaped tablespoon milled
  flaxseeds/linseeds
10 g/1 heaped tablespoon
  mixed sesame seeds
15 g/1½ tablespoons mixed
  sunflower and pumpkin seeds
10 g/1 tablespoon desiccated/
  dried shredded coconut
5 g/1 tablespoon goji berries
70 ml/⅓ cup hemp milk, or other
  milk of your choice

SERVES 1

Mix all the ingredients together in a container with a lid, cover and leave in the fridge overnight.

By morning, the seeds, coconut and berries will have plumped up with milk and can be enjoyed either at home or on the go. The mixture will keep for up to 3 days in the fridge.

Chia pot

15 g/1 tablespoon chia seeds
85 g/⅓ cup almond milk, or other
  milk of your choice
1 vanilla pod/bean (seeds only)
1 tablespoon almond butter
flaked/slivered almonds, to serve

SERVES 1

Mix all the ingredients together in a container with a lid, stir a few times in the first 30 minutes. Leave in the fridge overnight and enjoy in the morning.

Add some flaked/slivered almonds for added texture and serve. The mixture will keep for up to 3 days in the fridge.

Grainy porridge

50 g/¼ cup quinoa
100 g/½ cup amaranth
100 g/½ cup millet
a pinch of salt
450 ml/scant 2 cups almond,
    coconut, oat or other milk
    of your choice, plus extra
    if needed

GLOW BALLS
200 g/1½ cups Brazil nuts
100 g/¾ cup dates, pitted
100 g/¾ cup dried figs
1 tablespoon desiccated/
    dried shredded coconut
2 tablespoons coconut oil
½ teaspoon ground turmeric
½ teaspoon ground cinnamon
4 cardamom pods, ground
2 tablespoons ground
    flaxseeds/linseeds
1 tablespoon cocoa nibs
½ tablespoon bee pollen

WHIPPED HONEY
    VANILLA BUTTER
150 g/1¼ sticks salted butter,
    softened
1 teaspoon vanilla paste
2 tablespoons runny honey

TO SERVE
bee pollen
pumpkin seeds
goji berries
nuts
honey

MAKES 6 SMALL BOWLS
OR 3 LARGE BOWLS

This is an earthier version of traditional porridge, made using ancient grains.

First, make the glow balls. In a food processor place the Brazil nuts, dates, figs, shredded coconut, coconut oil, turmeric, cinnamon, cardamom and flaxseeds/linseeds, and blitz into a textured paste. Transfer into a bowl and mix in the cocoa nibs and bee pollen. Form into 40 balls and set aside in the fridge until needed.

Bring the quinoa, amaranth, millet, salt, milk and 450 ml/scant 2 cups water to the boil in a medium pan. Reduce the heat, partially cover and simmer, stirring occasionally, until the cereal is the consistency of porridge (softer and thicker than the usual bowl of oatmeal) and water is absorbed, for approximately 40–50 minutes. If you want a looser, creamier texture, add more milk at this stage.

Meanwhile, make the whipped honey vanilla butter. Place the softened butter, vanilla paste and honey in a bowl. Using a hand-held mixer, whisk the ingredients together until light and fluffy.

Serve the porridge sprinkled with bee pollen, some glow balls, whipped honey vanilla butter and with your choice of other toppings.

Spiced sweet potato porridge

Sweet potato is the perfect brunch ingredient because it is a slow-releasing carbohydrate, and the cinnamon here provides sweetness without adding sugar.

200 ml/¾ cup almond milk, or other milk of your choice
2 cinnamon sticks (or 1 teaspoon ground cinnamon), plus extra ground to serve
10 cardamom pods
2 tablespoons pure maple syrup (optional)
150 g/1 cup grated sweet potato
a small handful of mixed nuts and sultanas/golden raisins
1 banana, sliced

SERVES 2

Put the almond milk, cinnamon, cardamom pods and maple syrup, if using, in a saucepan set over medium heat and bring to a gentle simmer. Turn the heat right down so that the milk stays warm and the flavours can infuse for at least 10 minutes. Turn off the heat and cool completely before straining into a jug/pitcher using a fine-mesh sieve/strainer. You could prepare this in advance and store the infused milk in the fridge so it's ready for you to use when required.

Return the infused milk to the pan. Bring to a gentle simmer, add the grated sweet potato and cook for 15–20 minutes, stirring often, or until the potato has softened. Add the nuts and sultanas/golden raisins and stir through.

To serve, pour into bowls, top with sliced banana and sprinkle with a little ground cinnamon.

Quinoa granola
with tropical fruit & coconut yogurt

150 g/1 cup quinoa granola
  (see below)
150 g/3½ oz. (about ¼) papaya,
  washed and cut into shards
150 g/3½ oz. pineapple, peeled,
  cored and cut into shards
150 g/3½ oz. mango, washed
  and cut into shards
2 passion fruits, halved
200 g/1 cup coconut yogurt
coconut blossom syrup, to serve

QUINOA GRANOLA
200 g/2 cups quinoa flakes
2 tablespoons ground
  flaxseeds/linseeds
1 tablespoon chia seeds
  (optional)
50 g/scant ½ cup macadamia
  nuts, roughly chopped
50 g/scant ½ cup pistachio nuts,
  roughly chopped
50 g/scant ½ cup cashew nuts,
  roughly chopped
4 tablespoons coconut
  blossom syrup
1 tablespoon apple juice
1 teaspoon vanilla paste
30 g/¾ cup coconut chips,
  lightly toasted

*a baking sheet lined with
  baking parchment*

SERVES 6

A nourishing gluten- and refined sugar-free granola, served on coconut yogurt with a colourful selection of tropical fruit.

Preheat the oven to 180°C (350°F) Gas 4.

For the quinoa granola, put the quinoa flakes, ground flaxseeds/linseeds, chia seeds (if using) and the nuts in a large bowl and mix together. Stir in the coconut blossom syrup, apple juice and vanilla paste. Spread the mixture onto the prepared baking sheet and bake in the preheated oven for 10 minutes. Break up the mixture with a fork and bake for another 10 minutes. Remove from the oven and stir in the coconut chips. Allow to cool. Store in an airtight container for up to a month (this keeps well so you may wish to double up on the quantities).

To serve, arrange the fruit on a serving plates. Spoon some granola into a bowl or glass, top with coconut yogurt and serve with a little pot of coconut blossom syrup alongside.

Honey & vanilla granola

Granola is the ultimate wellbeing breakfast and you can, of course, vary the ingredients to include your preferred breakfast flavours. Here are some classic additions such as ground ginger, pumpkin seeds and dried cranberries. This recipe makes a large quantity and as it keeps for up to a month, it's ideal to prepare in advance when planning brunch for a crowd.

250 g/1 cup clear honey
1 teaspoon vanilla paste,
  or 1 vanilla pod/bean,
  (seeds only)
450 g/3½ cups rolled/
  old-fashioned oats
300 g/2¼ cups barley or
  millet flakes
50 g/½ cup soya/soy bran
½ teaspoon ground ginger
70 g/⅔ cup pumpkin seeds
70 g/⅔ cup sunflower seeds
70 g/1 cup rice puffs
  (brown or white)
90 g/⅔ cup chopped dried
  fruit, such as apricots,
  cranberries, figs, raspberries
  or a combination

To Serve
natural/plain yogurt
honey, to drizzle

*a baking sheet lined with
  baking parchment*

Makes 30–40 servings

Preheat the oven to 120°C (250°F) Gas ½.

Put the honey in a cup and stir in the vanilla paste or seeds. In a separate bowl, mix together the oats, barley or millet flakes, soya/soy bran and ginger together. Spread out the granola mixture on the prepared baking sheet. Drizzle the honey mixture over the granola as evenly as possible, trying to cover it all. Bake in the preheated oven for about 40 minutes, or until it is a light golden colour.

Tip the granola into a bowl and stir in the rest of the ingredients. Once cooled, serve or store in an airtight container for up to 1 month.

Serve the granola with a generous dollop of yogurt and a drizzle of honey.

Super berry granola

Super berries — such as açai, goji, inca/golden, cranberries and blueberries, to name a few — have been hailed as anti-ageing superfoods due to their high levels of antioxidants and vitamins that help to keep your skin glowing. Nowadays you can buy mixed bags of these super berries and can add them to your homemade granola every morning.

300 g/3 cups gluten-free or steel-cut oats
70 g/½ cup flaked/slivered almonds
75 g/1 cup desiccated/dried shredded coconut
80 g/½ cup chia seeds
70 g/½ cup pumpkin seeds
70 g/½ cup sunflower seeds
a pinch of salt
125 g/scant ½ cup honey, plus extra to serve
125 ml/½ cup algae, coconut or sunflower oil
150 g/1 cup mixed dried super berries
natural/plain yogurt, to serve

a baking sheet lined with baking parchment

SERVES 8–10

Preheat the oven to 150°C (300°F) Gas 2.

Put the oats, almonds, coconut, chia, pumpkin and sunflower seeds, plus a pinch of salt, in a large mixing bowl and give it a good stir together. Drizzle the honey and oil over the top and stir in. Once the mixture starts clumping together and everything is coated in honey and oil, spread it out on the prepared baking sheet and cook in the preheated oven for 30 minutes. Give the granola a couple of stirs while it's cooking to make sure everything is evenly baked. It will be a lovely golden colour and crisp texture when cooked.

Remove from the oven and allow to cool.

Once cooled, stir in the super berries and store in an airtight container for up to 2 weeks. Serve with yogurt and a drizzle of extra honey, if desired.

Baked oat milk porridge
with pears, almonds & date syrup

You might wonder why anyone would oven-bake porridge, when it takes so little time to cook the conventional way? Well, it does mean that you can swap standing at the stove and stirring constantly for simply mixing everything together and leaving it to morph into breakfast heaven under its own steam, while you soak in the bath or even go back to bed with your book!

160 g/1¾ cups jumbo oats
1.2 litres/5 cups oat milk
75 g/½ cup mixed seeds
2 teaspoons vanilla bean paste
1 teaspoon ground cinnamon
3 medium ripe, but firm pears, cored and diced
80 g/⅔ cup mixed dried berries (sultanas/golden raisins, goji berries, inca/golden berries, cranberries, etc.)

To Serve
2 tablespoons toasted flaked/slivered almonds
4–5 tablespoons date syrup
extra oat milk

Serves 4–6

Preheat the oven to 170°C (325°F) Gas 3. Mix the oats and oat milk together. Stir in the seeds, vanilla bean paste, ground cinnamon, diced pears and dried berries. Pour everything into a roasting pan, cover with foil and bake for 30 minutes. Remove from the oven and spoon into bowls. Scatter with the toasted almonds and drizzle with date syrup and extra oat milk as desired. Serve at once.

Melon & raspberry salad in stem ginger syrup

Ginger and melon are quite simply a match made in culinary heaven. The sweetness of one sets off the sharpness of the other one and vice versa. Make this when melons are bursting with ripe perfume and the raspberries are as sweet as can be.

100 g/½ cup light brown sugar
50 g/2 oz. stem ginger, drained and
    finely chopped
juice of 1 lemon
1 charentais or Cantaloupe melon,
    peeled and deseeded
200 g/1¼ cups raspberries

SERVES 4

Put the light brown sugar in a saucepan with the ginger and 200 ml/¾ cup water. Heat gently until the sugar has completely dissolved, then turn up the heat and simmer for 5 minutes. Remove from the heat and add the lemon juice. Let cool.

Slice or chop the melon, place in a bowl and pour over the cooled syrup. Tumble over the raspberries, then serve.

Orange-baked rhubarb

Rhubarb has a finite season so make the most of it whilst it is around. Rhubarb and orange are delightful together and make for a fine brunch dish. The flavours work exceedingly well with something creamy alongside, such as coconut milk yogurt.

400 g/14 oz. rhubarb, rinsed and
    cut into 5-cm/2-in. pieces
zest and freshly squeezed juice
    of 1 orange
1½ tablespoons honey
coconut milk yogurt, to serve

SERVES 4

Preheat the oven to 180°C (350°F) Gas 4.

Put the rhubarb on a sheet pan with sides. Squeeze over the orange juice and add the zest, then drizzle over the honey and stir everything together.

Bake in the preheated oven for 30 minutes until the rhubarb is soft. Stir once or twice during baking time.

Serve with a generous dollop of yogurt.

Roasted apricots with goat's curd puddles & oat clusters

Goat's curd is a glorious thing — smooth and creamy, with a perfect suggestion of lemon. Combine it with juicy summer apricots, add a crumbly oat and almond topping, bake until bubbling and you have bliss in a breakfast bowl (unless you're having it for dessert, which happens to work beautifully too).

500 g/18 oz. fresh ripe, but firm apricots
2 tablespoons thick honey, plus extra to serve
30 g/2 tablespoons softened butter
45 g/½ cup jumbo oats
30 g/scant ½ cup flaked/slivered almonds
20 g/1 tablespoon plus 2 teaspoons light brown muscovado sugar
300 g/10½ oz. goat's curd

SERVES 4

Preheat the oven to 180°C (350°F) Gas 4.

Cut the apricots in half horizontally, remove the pits and arrange on a large sheet pan. Drizzle the honey over. Rub the butter, oats, flaked/slivered almonds and sugar together until the butter is evenly incorporated. Scatter the mixture over the apricots and roast for about 25 minutes, until the oat clusters are golden. Remove the pan from the oven and spoon little puddles of goat's curd here and there. Bake for a further 8–10 minutes, until the curd is melted and has little golden patches.

Serve straight from the pan and drizzle with more honey, to taste.

Pancakes & Waffles

Gluten-free apple pancakes

Sweet potato pancakes with cinnamon & vanilla

Maple & bacon pancakes

Mushroom, bacon & onion pancakes

Banana pancakes with crispy Parma ham

Buttermilk blini pancakes with salmon & horseradish cream

Apple & blueberry waffles

Pork sausage & leek waffle with split pea 'syrup'

Pulled pork and Cheddar hotcakes

Cherry & ricotta blintzes with sour cherry soup

Banana bread French toast

French toast à la vanille

Gluten-free apple pancakes

150 g/1 heaping cup gluten-free
    plain/all-purpose flour
100 g/¾ cup buckwheat flour
1 tablespoon caster/
    granulated sugar
1 teaspoon gluten-free
    baking powder
a pinch of salt
1 egg
220 ml/scant 1 cup milk
½ teaspoon vanilla paste
butter, for frying
1 Granny Smith apple, cored,
    peeled and sliced into circles

To Serve
maple syrup
yogurt
vanilla powder
blackberries

Serves 4

These are quick to make and will be enjoyed by everyone, not just your gluten-free guests. The combination of the light nuttiness of the buckwheat, the tartness of the apple and the mellow sweetness of the maple syrup is a winner.

Put the flours, sugar, baking powder and salt in a bowl and make a well in the centre. Crack the egg in the middle and pour in one-quarter of the milk. Use a whisk to combine the mixture thoroughly. Once you have a paste, mix in another quarter of the milk and, when all the lumps are gone, mix in the remaining milk and the vanilla paste. Leave to rest for 20 minutes. Stir again before cooking.

Heat a small non-stick frying pan/skillet and add a knob/pat of butter. When the butter starts to foam, ladle the pancake mixture into the centre of the pan forming a circle, then place an apple ring in the centre. Cook for a few minutes until golden brown on the bottom and the bubbles are bursting on the surface of the pancake, then turn over and cook until golden on the other side. Repeat until you have used all the mixture, stirring the mixture between pancakes and adding more butter for frying as necessary.

Serve immediately with maple syrup, yogurt, vanilla powder and blackberries.

Sweet potato pancakes
with cinnamon & vanilla

These are pancakes with a difference as they contain sweet potato, their flavour enhanced by a hint of cinnamon and vanilla. The batter can be mixed the night before, which makes for a very relaxed weekend brunch.

300 g/10 oz. sweet potato, peeled and chopped
125 g/1 cup plain/all-purpose flour
1 teaspoon baking powder
1 teaspoon ground cinnamon
3–4 tablespoons caster/granulated sugar
1 tablespoon vanilla extract
125 ml/½ cup milk
1 egg, beaten
1 tablespoon butter, melted and slightly cooled
vegetable or groundnut oil, for frying

To Serve
yogurt
stewed apples
maple syrup

Serves 4–6

Bring a pan of water to the boil and steam the sweet potatoes until tender, then drain and leave to cool.

Meanwhile, sift the flour, baking powder and cinnamon into a large mixing bowl. Stir in the sugar. In a separate bowl, add the vanilla extract to the milk and egg, along with the melted butter. Gradually add the wet ingredients to the dry, combining it all together with a fork. The batter can be made up to 24 hours in advance and stored in the fridge in a bowl, covered, if you like.

To cook the pancakes, mash the sweet potatoes, then stir them through the batter until well combined. Melt a little oil in a non-stick frying pan/skillet over a fairly high heat. Once hot, carefully add heaped tablespoons of the batter. Gently fry until golden brown on both sides, turning them with a spatula.

Serve stacked with yogurt, stewed apples and maple syrup for a hearty breakfast.

Maple & bacon pancakes

What's not to like about the well-loved combination of pancakes, bacon and maple syrup? Here is a classic version of the popular sweet 'n' salty brunch-time treat.

125 g/1 cup plain/
　all-purpose flour
2 teaspoons caster/
　granulated sugar
1½ teaspoons baking powder
½ teaspoon bicarbonate of/
　baking soda
½ teaspoon salt
310 ml/1¼ cups buttermilk
2 tablespoons unsalted butter,
　melted
1 egg
10 slices of streaky/fatty bacon
maple syrup, to serve (optional)

MAKES 10 PANCAKES

Preheat the oven to 200°C (400°F) Gas 6.

In a bowl, whisk together the flour, sugar, baking powder, bicarbonate of/baking soda and salt. In another bowl, whisk together the buttermilk, butter and egg. Mix the flour mixture into the buttermilk mixture until just combined, with small to medium lumps remaining.

In a large non-stick frying pan/skillet, fry the bacon until golden on both sides and just turning crisp. Drain the bacon on paper towels and set aside.

Make each bacon pancake by dropping a tablespoon of batter into the pan/skillet, top with a bacon rasher/slice, and cover with a further teaspoon of batter. Cook until some bubbles appear on top of the pancake and a few have burst, 1½–2 minutes. With a spatula, carefully flip the pancake and cook until golden. Repeat with all the bacon rashers/slices, cooking in batches if necessary and keeping the cooked pancakes warm in a low oven. Make more pancakes in the same way with any remaining batter, adding more oil to the pan if necessary. Serve with maple syrup if desired.

Mushroom, bacon & onion pancakes

Starting your weekend with a proper breakfast or a late brunch always feels like a treat. These small, fluffy pancakes — flavoured with mushrooms, bacon and onion — make a great savoury all-in-one brunch dish to enjoy. Make a tall stack of them and share with friends.

½ tablespoon sunflower oil

3 slices of bacon, cut into short strips

½ onion, finely chopped

100 g/3½ oz. button mushrooms, halved

225 g/1½ cups plain/all-purpose flour

1 tablespoon baking powder

½ teaspoon salt

2 eggs

200 ml/1 scant cup milk

1 tablespoon freshly chopped parsley

1 tablespoon freshly snipped chives

25 g/2 tablespoons butter, melted

maple syrup, to serve (optional)

SERVES 4–6

Heat the sunflower oil in a frying pan/skillet. Fry the bacon and onion for 2 minutes, stirring. Add the mushrooms and fry over a high heat until lightly browned. Set aside to cool.

Sift the flour, baking powder and salt into a mixing bowl. Break the eggs into the centre of the flour and pour in the milk, folding the ingredients together quickly, without over-mixing, to form a thick batter. Gently fold in the mushroom mixture, parsley and chives. Stir in the melted butter.

Thoroughly heat a large, heavy-based frying pan/skillet. Dry fry the mixture in batches, using a tablespoon of the batter to form each small pancake. Fry for 2–3 minutes over a low–medium heat, until the pancakes have set and begun to dry out around the edges. Using a spatula, gently turn them over and fry for a further 2 minutes until golden brown on both sides. Serve at once with maple syrup, if you like.

Banana pancakes
with crispy Parma ham

This pancake recipe uses Parma ham rather than bacon and makes the perfect weekend breakfast, with a hit of sweet and savoury to set your taste buds alight.

2 bananas, mashed

2 eggs

1 teaspoon vanilla bean paste (or the seeds from 1 vanilla pod/bean)

1 teaspoon ground cinnamon

2 tablespoons vanilla protein powder

1 tablespoon chia seeds

coconut oil (or coconut butter), for frying

To Serve
Parma or prosciutto ham
maple syrup
flaked/slivered almonds

Serves 2

Mix all of the ingredients together well in a large mixing bowl and set aside for 10–15 minutes so the chia seeds plump up and turn a little gelatinous – adding them here helps to thicken the batter.

Set a non-stick frying pan/skillet over a low–medium heat and add a little coconut oil or coconut butter. Cooking these pancakes over low–medium heat keeps them soft and springy. However, always make sure the pan is heated before adding the batter or the pancakes won't hold their shape and will become flat.

Cook the pancakes in batches of two or three. Pour even spoonfuls of the batter into the pan and when the bubbles start to form on top, they should be ready to flip. Turn over using a spatula and cook the other side of each pancake.

Remove from the pan, turn up the heat and crisp up the Parma or prosciutto ham.

Serve the pancakes in stacks with a drizzle of maple syrup and topped with a sprinkle of flaked/slivered almonds and crispy Parma or prosciutto ham.

Buttermilk blini pancakes
with salmon & horseradish cream

Blini pancakes topped with smoked salmon make fantastic breakfast canapés. For a more indulgent version, why not serve large, fluffy buttermilk pancakes seasoned with chives, and topped with thick slices of smoked salmon and horseradish cream? As well as a brunch dish, smaller blinis or larger pancakes are great as a light lunch or supper too.

170 g/1⅓ cups self-raising/
   self-rising flour, sifted
1 teaspoon baking powder
2 eggs, separated
200 ml/⅔ cup buttermilk
2 teaspoons caster/
   granulated sugar
1 tablespoon finely snipped
   chives, plus extra
   for sprinkling
100 ml/⅓ cup milk
250 ml/1 cup crème fraîche
1 heaped tablespoon creamed
   horseradish
1–2 tablespoons butter,
   for frying
salt and freshly ground
   black pepper

To Serve
400 g/2½ cups smoked salmon
1 lemon, sliced into wedges

Serves 4

To make the pancake batter, put the flour, baking powder, egg yolks, buttermilk, sugar and chives in a large mixing bowl and whisk together. Season well with salt and pepper, then gradually add the milk until the batter is smooth and pourable.

In a separate bowl, whisk the egg whites to stiff peaks. Gently fold the whisked egg whites into the batter mixture using a spatula. Cover the bowl and put in the fridge to rest for 30 minutes.

For the horseradish cream, whisk together the crème fraîche and horseradish in a small bowl and season with salt and pepper.

When you are ready to serve, remove the batter mixture from the fridge and stir once. Put a little butter in a large frying pan/skillet set over a medium heat. Allow the butter to melt and coat the base of the pan, then ladle small amounts of the rested batter into the pan, leaving a little space between each. Cook until the underside of each pancake is golden brown and a few bubbles start to appear on the top – this will take about 2–3 minutes. Turn the pancake over using a spatula and cook on the other side until golden brown.

Serve the pancakes warm, topped with slices of smoked salmon, a generous spoon of the horseradish cream and a wedge of lemon to squeeze over the top. Sprinkle with extra snipped chives.

Apple & blueberry waffles

Waffles are a great breakfast or brunch treat, and this spiced recipe is a refreshing diversion from the usual flavour combinations associated with them. Do not add too much fat, sugar or egg to the waffle mixture, or they will go soft soon after cooking.

1 vanilla pod/bean
250 ml/1 cup milk
250 g/2 cups plain/
    all-purpose flour, sifted
2 teaspoons baking powder
½ teaspoon salt
½ teaspoon ground cardamom
    (optional)
2 tablespoons sugar
200 g/13 tablespoons butter
250 ml/1 cup whipping cream
6 eggs, beaten

Apple & Blueberry Topping
1 large apple
150 g/1 heaping cup blueberries
½ a cinnamon stick
1 star anise
2 whole cloves
300 ml/1⅓ cups pomegranate,
    grape or cranberry juice

To Serve
vanilla yogurt

a waffle iron

Makes 12

To make the waffles, split the vanilla pod/bean in half lengthways, then put it in a small pan with the milk, heat gently and set aside for at least 30 minutes.

In a bowl, mix all the dry ingredients together. Melt the butter in a small pan. Add the butter and infused milk (discard the pod/bean), with the cream and eggs, to the dry ingredients and whisk lightly until a batter consistency is formed. Leave the batter to rest for around 30 minutes, or overnight in the fridge if possible.

Meanwhile, make the topping. Remove the core from the apple and slice it, keeping the skin on. Place the apple, along with the other topping ingredients, in a pan and cook until the apple and blueberries are soft, about 3–4 minutes. Remove the fruit with a slotted spoon and set aside. Boil the remaining juices for 10–15 minutes, until a syrup consistency is reached. Strain the syrup to remove the spices, then return it to the pan to cook gently for a further 2 minutes, with the fruit. You can then blend the mixture if you like, or keep the fruit whole.

Heat a waffle iron over a medium heat. Spoon the mixture into the iron, just up to the top. Cook the waffle until it is a golden colour, then remove and cool on a wire rack until ready to serve. To serve, pour the fruit over the waffles, adding a blob of vanilla yogurt, and a spoonful of the apple topping.

Pork sausage & leek waffle
with split pea 'syrup'

1 large russet potato, pricked
   with a fork
1/2 tablespoon vegetable oil
1 large leek, white and light
   green parts sliced and rinsed
125 ml/1/2 cup full-fat/whole milk
2 tablespoons sour cream
2 eggs
20 g/1/4 cup coarsely grated
   Parmesan cheese
40 g/1/4 cup plain/
   all-purpose flour
21/2 teaspoons baking powder
225 g/1/2 lb. pork sausage, cooked
   and crumbled (reserve the fat
   and set aside)
salt and ground white pepper
non-stick spray, for greasing

SPLIT PEA 'SYRUP'
225 g/1 1/4 cups green split peas
1 onion, peeled, sliced
1 leek, white part only, sliced
1 teaspoon dried mint, crushed
1 teaspoon dried marjoram,
   crushed
1/2 teaspoon salt
1/4–1/2 teaspoon freshly ground
   black pepper
1 tablespoon white vinegar
3 tablespoons butter mixed with
   reserved sausage drippings

a waffle iron

SERVES 4

This sausage and leek waffle is a savoury take on one of the world's most beloved breakfast items. Serve alongside a split pea 'syrup', which is really not a syrup, but a split pea purée.

Preheat the oven to 200°C (400°F) Gas 6.

Bake the potato in the preheated oven until soft, about 1 hour, turning once halfway through.

Meanwhile, make the split pea 'syrup'. Fill a large saucepan with 500 ml/2 cups water. Add the split peas, onion, leek, mint, marjoram, salt and black pepper. Simmer on low until the peas and onion are very tender, about 45 minutes. Remove from the heat and allow to cool slightly. Add the vinegar and purée in two batches in a blender or food processor. Transfer to a saucepan or pot and set aside.

Once the baked potato is cooked, scoop the cooked flesh out of the potato into a medium bowl and mash. Set aside. Discard the skin.

Heat the vegetable oil in a small frying pan/skillet over a medium heat. Add the leek and sauté until softened but not browned, about 4 minutes. Season with salt and white pepper. Remove from the heat.

Add the leeks, milk and sour cream to the potato and whisk together. Whisk in the eggs and cheese. Whisk in the flour and baking powder until a thick batter is formed. Let rest.

Heat a waffle iron and coat with non-stick spray. Pour the batter into the waffle iron and top with the crumbled, cooked sausage. Cook until lightly browned. Keep warm in a low oven while other waffles cook. Reheat the split pea purée.

Serve the warm waffles with the split pea purée poured over, or serve it alongside to dip.

Pulled pork & Cheddar hotcakes

Pork and Cheddar hotcakes put a spin on the old ham and cheese sandwich. This fluffy pancake batter is sprinkled with roasted pork belly or leftover cooked pulled pork, Cheddar and a little dill for extra flavour. Serve with or without the syrup, depending whether you fancy a hit of sweetness, or prefer to keep things savoury.

520 g/4 cups plain/
   all-purpose flour
1 teaspoon salt
4 teaspoons baking powder
500 ml/2 cups milk
500 ml/2 cups buttermilk
2 eggs
300 g/2 cups cooked pulled
   pork or cooked pork belly,
   as preferred
270 g/3 cups grated/shredded
   Cheddar cheese
a handful of freshly chopped
   dill (optional)
butter, for frying and serving
maple syrup, to serve

SERVES 4

Stir together the flour, salt and baking powder. Add the milk, buttermilk and eggs and stir well with an egg-beater or whisk until there are no lumps. Cover and let rest in the fridge for 30–60 minutes.

To make the pancakes, heat about ½ tablespoon of butter in a non-stick or cast-iron frying pan/skillet over a medium-high heat. Add about 80 ml/⅓ cup of the batter and smooth out with ladle or spoon to make a circle.

Sprinkle with a few tablespoons of pork, about 20 g/¼ cup grated/shredded cheese and a sprinkle of dill, if using. Drizzle a bit more batter over the top. When the batter forms large bubbles, flip the pancake over and continue cooking until cooked through.

Remove and keep warm while you cook the remaining pancakes. Use a little butter in the pan for every pancake, or as needed. Serve hot with butter and syrup.

Cherry & ricotta blintzes with sour cherry soup

Blintzes are pancakes without any raising agent, similar to a crêpe. This recipe is accompanied by a cold sour cherry soup.

375 ml/1½ cups semi-skimmed/
   skim milk
3 eggs
30 g/2 tablespoons butter,
   melted
90 g/²/₃ cup plain/
   all-purpose flour
½ teaspoon salt

SOUR CHERRY SOUP
340 g/³/₄ lb. sweet, dark cherries,
   stoned/pitted (save the
   stones/pits for the recipe)
50 g/¼ cup sugar
60 ml/¼ cup red wine
½ teaspoon salt
1 tablespoon finely grated
   lemon zest
100 g/½ cup Greek yogurt

CHEESE FILLING
225 g/1 cup ricotta cheese
85 g/3 oz. cream cheese,
   softened
50 g/¼ cup sugar
½ teaspoon vanilla extract

CHERRY SAUCE
450 g/1 lb. fresh or frozen
   pitted cherries
50 g/¼ cup sugar
1 tablespoon cornflour/
   cornstarch

*20-cm/8-inch non-stick frying
   pan/skillet, lightly greased
greased baking tin/pan*

SERVES 4

To make the soup, place the cherry stones/pits in a large saucepan. Add 600 ml/2½ cups water, bring to the boil, then simmer for 5 minutes. Remove the stones/pits. Add the sugar, wine, salt and zest and bring back to the boil. Boil for 3 minutes. Add the cherries, cover and simmer 5 minutes. Remove from the heat and set aside. In a large bowl whisk the yogurt with 125 ml/½ cup of the the soup until the mixture is smooth. Slowly add the rest of the soup, and whisk until smooth. Allow to cool, stirring from time to time, then refrigerate until cold.

In a small bowl, combine the milk, eggs and butter. Set aside. In another small or medium bowl, combine the flour and salt together by whisking. Add the flour and salt mixture into the milk mixture and combine. Cover and refrigerate for 2 hours.

Heat the frying pan/skillet. Pour 2 tablespoons of batter into the centre, tilting the pan to coat it evenly. Cook until the top appears dry. Using a small spatula, turn it over and cook for 15–20 seconds longer. Remove to a wire rack to cool. Repeat with the remaining batter. Stack the cooled crêpes with waxed paper or paper towels in between, wrap in foil and refrigerate.

Preheat the oven to 180°C (350°F) Gas 4.

To make the filling, in a blender or food processor, process the ricotta until smooth. Transfer to a bowl, add the cream cheese and beat until smooth. Beat in the sugar and vanilla. Spread 1 rounded tablespoonful onto each crêpe. Fold the opposite sides of the crêpe over the filling. Place seam-side down in the greased baking pan. Repeat with the remaining crêpes. Bake, uncovered, in the preheated oven for 10 minutes.

For the sauce, bring the cherries, sugar and 160 ml/²/₃ cup water to the boil in a large pan over medium heat, then cover and simmer for 5 minutes. Mix the cornflour/cornstarch with 1 tablespoon water into a smooth paste, then stir into the pan. Bring to the boil and cook for 2 minutes, stirring constantly. Serve slightly warm with the hot blintzes and the cold soup.

Banana bread French toast

French toast in itself is a decadent brunch, but using banana bread really jazzes up this morning treat. Feel free to use caramel sauce or clear honey instead of maple syrup.

BANANA BREAD
280 g/2 cups plain/
    all-purpose flour
1 teaspoon baking powder
¼ teaspoon salt
115 g/1 stick butter
150 g/¾ cup brown sugar
2 eggs, beaten
5 ripe, mashed bananas

FRENCH TOAST
3 eggs
3 tablespoons sweetened
    condensed milk
1 teaspoon vanilla extract
    or paste
2 tablespoons butter
icing/confectioners' sugar,
    for dusting
maple syrup, to serve

a 23 x 13-cm/9 x 5-inch loaf pan,
    lightly greased

SERVES 4

Preheat an oven to 180°C (350°F) Gas 4.

Make the banana bread by combining the flour, baking powder and salt in a large mixing bowl. In a separate medium bowl, cream together the butter and brown sugar. Stir the eggs in one at a time and add the mashed bananas until combined. Add the banana mixture to the flour mixture and stir with a wooden spoon until mixed together. Pour into the prepared loaf pan. Bake in the preheated oven for 1 hour, or until a cocktail stick/toothpick inserted into the centre comes out clean. Let cool for 5–10 minutes and then turn it out onto a wire rack.

For the French toast, beat the eggs, sweetened condensed milk and vanilla with a fork in a small-medium bowl. Set aside.

Melt the butter in a large frying pan/skillet over a medium heat. Slice the banana bread into 4 thick slices. Dip each slice into the egg mixture and place into the hot frying pan/skillet. Cook on each side for 1–2 minutes until golden brown. Plate and dust with icing/confectioners' sugar. Serve with a side of maple syrup.

French toast à la vanille

Oozing with a wonderfully rich vanilla aroma, this version of French toast makes for one decadent brunch. It's quick and simple to make, and perfect to tuck into on a slow Sunday morning.

2 UK large/US extra-large eggs
a dash of milk
1 teaspoon vanilla extract
1 teaspoon olive oil
4 slices fresh thick white bread

To Serve
1 lemon, cut into wedges
fresh berries
sugar
ground cinnamon (optional)

Serves 4

Crack the eggs into a wide bowl, add the milk and vanilla extract and whisk it all together. Heat the oil in a frying pan/skillet over a medium-high heat. Dip the bread slices in the egg mixture and place them in the pan. Cook for a couple of minutes, turning the pieces over so they are golden brown on both sides.

Serve with a squeeze of lemon and fresh berries spooned over, sugar to sprinkle and a dusting of ground cinnamon, if liked. Add a lovely glass of freshly squeezed orange juice or your morning espresso – and relax!

Eggs & Brunch Plates

Scrambled eggs with chanterelles

Baked mushroom & egg ramekins

Breakfast tart

Sweet potato, spinach & red onion frittata

Simple baked eggs with chorizo cornbread

Smoked salmon big breakfast

Fisherman's Wharf Benedict on sourdough

Fried green tomato Benedict

Paris-style eggs Benedict

Posh fish finger sandwich & homemade tartare sauce

Steak & egg breakfast tacos

Spinach, artichoke & goats' cheese pizza

Triple meat & Cheddar breakfast quiche

Tomato bacon gratin

Scrambled eggs with chanterelles

This simple but luxurious combination makes a wonderful breakfast or brunch dish.

100 g/3½ oz. fresh
  chanterelle mushrooms
4 eggs
1 tablespoon butter, plus
  extra for the toast
1 tablespoon olive oil
2 slices of freshly made toast
salt and freshly ground
  black pepper
freshly chopped parsley,
  to garnish (optional)

SERVES 2

Trim down the stalks of the chanterelle mushrooms and halve any large ones.

Beat the eggs together in a bowl and season with salt and pepper. Heat the butter in small, heavy saucepan. Add the beaten eggs and cook over a low heat, stirring often, until just scrambled.

Meanwhile, heat the olive oil in a frying pan/skillet. Add the chanterelles and fry over a high heat for 2–3 minutes, until lightly browned and softened. Season with salt and pepper.

Spread the toast with butter, top with the scrambled eggs and then the fried chanterelles. Serve at once, garnished with freshly chopped parsley.

Baked mushroom & egg ramekins

Mushrooms and eggs have a delicious affinity – their delicate flavours complementing each other, rather than overpowering. This traditional egg dish is given a luxurious touch by adding a layer of fried mushrooms. A hint of tarragon adds a pleasing aniseed note. Serve with thick slices of fresh bread.

1 tablespoon olive oil
½ onion, finely chopped
400 g/14 oz. white/cup
  mushrooms, thinly sliced
2 tablespoons freshly chopped
  tarragon leaves, plus extra
  to garnish
4 eggs
4 tablespoons double/
  heavy cream
4 tablespoons grated
  Parmesan cheese
salt and freshly ground
  black pepper

4 ramekin dishes

SERVES 4

Preheat the oven to 180°C (350°F) Gas 4.

Heat the olive oil in a frying pan/skillet. Fry the onion over a low heat, until softened. Add the mushrooms, increase the heat, and fry briefly until the mushrooms are softened. Mix in the tarragon, season with salt and freshly ground black pepper, and cook for a further 2 minutes.

Divide the mushroom mixture evenly between the ramekin dishes.

Break an egg into the centre of each ramekin. Season the eggs with salt and pepper. Pour a tablespoon of double/heavy cream over each egg, then sprinkle each with Parmesan cheese.

Bake in the preheated oven for 8–10 minutes for runny yolks, or 15–20 minutes for set yolks. Serve warm from the oven, garnished with extra tarragon.

Breakfast tart

When constructing this tart, it is important to create a good dam, or well, for the egg to sit in to prevent any spillages. When you arrange the first layer of leeks, create the wells and reinforce them with the pancetta — serious building skills are required here!

50 g/3½ tablespoons butter, roughly chopped
1 leek, thinly sliced
1 garlic clove, finely chopped
2 tablespoons roughly chopped thyme and oregano (or 1 teaspoon each of dried thyme and oregano)
8 filo/phyllo pastry sheets
10 slices of pancetta
6 eggs
1 tablespoon olive oil
1½ handfuls of rocket/arugula, coarsely chopped
tomato chutney, to serve (optional, see pages 126–129)

a 20 x 29-cm/8 x 11½-inch baking sheet

SERVES 4–6

Preheat the oven to 180°C (350°F) Gas 4.

Melt half the butter in a large frying pan/skillet over a medium heat, add the leek and garlic and stir occasionally until starting to caramelize. Add the herbs to the pan and set aside off the heat.

Melt the remaining butter and brush the base and sides of the baking sheet. Trim the filo/phyllo pastry sheets to fit the inside the baking sheet. Place the first pastry sheet on the baking sheet, brush with butter, then lay over another pastry sheet and repeat until all the pastry is used.

Spread the leek mixture over the pastry base. Make six evenly spaced indentations in the leek mixture. Place the pancetta over the tart, leaving the indentations free for the eggs. Place in the preheated oven for 7 minutes.

Crack the eggs into the indentations, drizzle with oil and bake until the tart is set and the eggs are medium cooked (approximately 10–15 minutes). Scatter over the rocket/arugula and return to the oven until just wilted. Serve with a tomato chutney, if you like.

Sweet potato, spinach & red onion frittata

This delicious frittata is packed with goodness. As well as being a healthy brunch dish, it can also be served cold, making it a great picnic dish.

1 sweet potato, peeled and sliced into 1-cm/½-inch rounds
150 g/3 cups baby spinach leaves
1–2 tablespoons olive oil, for frying
1 red onion, sliced
2 garlic cloves, finely chopped
½ teaspoon ground turmeric
6 eggs
salt and freshly ground black pepper
a mixed leaf salad, to serve (optional)

SERVES 4–6

Put the sweet potato slices in a saucepan and cover with water. Bring to the boil over a medium heat, then reduce the heat and leave to simmer for 7–8 minutes, or until soft all the way through. Drain and put in a bowl.

Put the spinach in a saucepan of boiling water and cook for about 30 seconds, until wilted. Drain and rinse with cold water to suspend the cooking. Squeeze out any excess water when cool enough to handle, then add to the sweet potatoes.

Heat a little olive oil in an ovenproof frying pan/skillet over a low heat, add the onion, garlic and turmeric, and fry gently for 3–4 minutes, until the onion is soft. Add the onion to the sweet potato slices and gently fold everything together.

Add a little more olive oil to the same pan, whisk together the eggs with a pinch of salt and pepper, and pour one-third of it into the pan to create a layer of egg on the bottom. Wait for it to settle and cook slightly, then spoon the sweet potato mixture on top, followed by the rest of the eggs. Push the vegetables down so they're just about covered by the eggs and leave to cook for 2 minutes, still on a low heat.

Preheat a grill/broiler to medium–hot.

Put the pan under the grill/broiler to finish cooking the frittata for about 5 minutes. You will know it is cooked all the way through when it doesn't wobble in the middle. You can also push the top with a knife – if you see runny egg, it needs more time.

Once cooked all the way through, leave the frittata to sit in the pan for 5 minutes. Slice and serve up warm with a side salad if you like.

Simple baked eggs
with chorizo cornbread

The baked eggs in this sunny brunch couldn't be any easier to prepare. If you want to take things to a decadent level, you can add an indulgent dollop of mascarpone cheese to each ramekin before you add the eggs. Perfect served with thick slices of freshly baked chorizo cornbread for dipping into the egg yolks.

BAKED EGGS (PER PERSON)
3 tablespoons home-made (see page 81) or good-quality shop-bought tomato sauce
1–2 eggs
1 heaped teaspoon finely grated Parmesan cheese
salt and freshly ground black pepper

CHORIZO CORNBREAD
150 g/5½ oz. chorizo, finely diced
540 g/3¾ cups polenta/cornmeal
4 teaspoons bicarbonate of/baking soda
2 teaspoons salt
1–2 tablespoons sugar (optional)
750 ml/3 cups buttermilk
2 eggs
2 tablespoons tomato purée/paste
170 g/1½ sticks unsalted butter, melted
olive oil

CORNBREAD SERVES 8

Preheat the oven to 200°C (400°F) Gas 6.

To make the cornbread, place a 30-cm/12-inch ovenproof cast-iron frying pan/skillet onto a medium heat. Once hot, add the chorizo and fry until the red oils escape and the chorizo is browned around the edges. Remove the chorizo and set aside but leave the oil in the pan/skillet as you will need it later.

Mix together the polenta/cornmeal, bicarbonate of/baking soda, salt and sugar (if using) in a large bowl. In another bowl, combine the buttermilk, eggs, tomato purée/paste and butter.

Pour the wet ingredients onto the dry ingredients and stir well to combine. Add the chorizo pieces back in and stir again.

Put the pan/skillet back over a medium heat. You need about 2 tablespoons of oil at the bottom of the pan/skillet. If the chorizo didn't give off enough oil, add some olive oil. Once the oil is hot, pour in the batter and spread evenly with a spatula.

Transfer to the preheated oven and bake for 25–30 minutes until the top is golden brown and a skewer comes out clean when inserted into the middle. Leave to rest for 10–20 minutes before serving.

For the baked eggs, preheat the oven to 180°C (350°F) Gas 4.

Put the tomato sauce into a large single-serve ramekin and crack in the egg(s) on top of the sauce. Season with salt and black pepper, and sprinkle over some Parmesan cheese.

Transfer to the preheated oven and cook for 8–10 minutes. The egg white should be cooked through but the yolk(s) still soft. Serve with slices of chorizo cornbread.

Smoked salmon big breakfast

This delicious (and slightly fancy) dish elevates any salmon-based brunch to another level!

coconut butter or oil, for frying
225 g/8 oz. vine cherry tomatoes
1 large ripe avocado, halved,
    stoned/pitted and sliced
1 lemon, cut into wedges
250 g/9 oz. smoked salmon
lumpfish caviar, to serve
    (optional)

Blini Batter
60 g/²/₃ cup ground almonds
40 g/¹/₃ cup arrowroot flour
1 teaspoon baking powder
2 eggs, separated
200 ml/³/₄ cup hemp milk,
    or other milk of your choice
1 tablespoon freshly chopped
    dill, plus extra to garnish
1 tablespoon freshly chopped
    parsley
1 tablespoon freshly snipped
    chives, plus extra to garnish
salt and freshly ground
    black pepper

Serves 4

First, prepare the blini batter. Mix the ground almonds, arrowroot flour and baking powder together in a large mixing bowl. Make a well in the centre and add the egg yolks and hemp milk. Whisk together slowly to avoid any lumps. Add the herbs and mix in with a fork – they just stick to the whisk if you continue to whisk in. Season well and set aside.

Whisk the egg whites in a separate, clean glass or stainless steel mixing bowl to soft peaks. Fold the egg whites into the batter and rest for 10 minutes.

Set a non-stick frying pan/skillet over a low–medium heat, and use a small amount of oil (preferably coconut butter or coconut oil). You will have to cook the blinis in batches, and this mixture is enough to allow 2 per person. Pour a little batter into the pan and leave until small bubbles form on the top of each blini. Flip over with a spatula and cook on the other side. Keep warm while you cook the rest of the batter in the same way.

Set another pan with a little oil over medium heat to cook the vine tomatoes. Add the tomatoes (on their vines) to the pan and cook for 3–4 minutes until the bottoms blacken and caramelize. Remove from the heat and set aside.

When ready to serve, top each blini with avocado slices. Squeeze over a little lemon juice to stop it discolouring, then add slices of smoked salmon on top. Spoon the lumpfish caviar over the top (if using) and arrange the tomatoes on the plate. Finish with a grind of black pepper, a pinch of salt if required, a few sprigs of fresh dill and a few snipped fresh chives.

Fisherman's Wharf Benedict on sourdough

This take on the classic is an ode to San Francisco's famed Fisherman's Wharf. It uses goat's cheese and avocado (two other things California does well!).

8 slices of fresh sourdough
   bread
450 g/3 cups shredded/picked
   over good-quality crab meat,
   at room temperature
8 eggs
120 g/4 oz. goat's cheese,
   sliced into quarters
2 ripe avocados, halved,
   stoned/pitted and sliced

LEMON HOLLANDAISE SAUCE
6 egg yolks
finely grated zest of
   1 small lemon
2 tablespoons Dijon mustard
340 g/3 sticks unsalted butter,
   melted
½ teaspoon salt
⅛ teaspoon freshly ground
   black pepper
⅛ teaspoon paprika

a double boiler (optional)

SERVES 4

Make the lemon hollandaise sauce. In a small saucepan or pot set over a low heat, bring 5 cm/2 inches of water to a bare simmer. Place a metal bowl over the pot to form a bain-marie.

Add the yolks, zest and mustard to the bowl of the bain-marie and whisk constantly until the mixture is thickened and ribbons form when you pull the whisk away from the bowl, about 4–5 minutes. The yolks should double or triple in volume.

Slowly whisk or beat in the melted butter, stirring constantly. Once the butter is fully incorporated, add the salt, pepper and paprika and continue whisking for about 3 minutes, until thick. If the mixture is too thick, add a little hot water as needed. Adjust the seasoning to taste. Remove from the heat and set aside.

Preheat the oven to 230°C (450°F) Gas 8.

Arrange the slices of sourdough on a baking sheet in a single layer. Bake until toasted, about 5 minutes. Put the toasted bread on serving plates and top with crab, dividing evenly.

To poach the eggs, bring 2.5 cm/1 inch of water to the boil in a medium pan. Lower the heat so small bubbles form on the bottom of the pan and break to the surface only occasionally.

Crack the eggs into the water one at a time, holding the shells close to the water's surface and letting the eggs slide out gently. Poach the eggs, in two batches to keep them from crowding, 6 minutes for soft-cooked. Lift the eggs out with a slotted spoon, pat dry with a paper towel, and place an egg on each crab-topped sourdough slice.

Top each egg with 2–3 tablespoons of the lemon hollandaise (gently reheated if necessary), and top with the goat's cheese and sliced avocado and a dusting of paprika. Serve immediately.

Fried green tomato Benedict

Fried green tomatoes are a perfect summer dish, ideal for this seasonal variation on the classic dish.

3 or 4 large green tomatoes, thickly sliced (about 6 slices per tomato)
150 g/1 cup cornmeal/polenta
vegetable oil, for frying
8 eggs
8 slices of smoked ham, thinly sliced
salt and freshly ground black pepper

Spiced Hollandaise Sauce
80 ml/⅓ cup red wine vinegar
8–10 peppercorns
1 small bay leaf
1 teaspoon ground nutmeg
6 egg yolks
225 g/2 sticks unsalted butter, melted
1½ teaspoons salt, or to taste
½ teaspoon cayenne pepper

Serves 4

Make the spiced hollandaise sauce. In a small saucepan set over a low heat, combine the vinegar, peppercorns, bay leaf and nutmeg. Reduce the mixture to 4 tablespoons. Remove from the heat and strain the peppercorns and bay leaf. Set aside to cool.

Place the egg yolks in the bowl of a stand mixer fitted with the whisk attachment, and slowly beat in the cooled, reduced vinegar mixture. With the mixer running on medium-high, slowly drizzle in the melted butter until it has all been added. Whisk or beat in the salt and cayenne pepper. Set aside.

Sprinkle the tomato slices liberally on both sides with salt and a few turns of cracked black pepper. Dredge the tomatoes liberally in cornmeal/polenta, and pat them to fully and evenly coat. Set aside the tomatoes while you heat the oil.

Heat about 1 cm/½ inch of oil in a large frying pan/skillet set over a medium heat. When the oil is hot, fry the tomatoes until the crust is golden brown and crisp on both sides, about 2–3 minutes per side. Remove and place on a flat baking sheet and blot with paper towels.

To poach the eggs, bring 2.5 cm/1 inch of water to the boil in a medium pan. Lower the heat so that small bubbles form on the bottom of the pan and break to the surface only occasionally. Crack the eggs into the water one at a time, holding the shells close to the water's surface and letting the eggs slide out gently. Poach the eggs, in two batches to keep them from crowding, 6 minutes for soft-cooked. Lift the eggs out with a slotted spoon and pat dry with a paper towel.

Place slices of tomato on a plate, overlapping the slices slightly. Pile on two thin slices of ham, and top with two poached eggs. Spoon a tablespoonful or two of the hollandaise over the eggs. Repeat with the remaining portions. Serve immediately.

Paris-style eggs Benedict

This variant on a traditional French breakfast comes with bacon, Brie and poached eggs, all assembled on top of a pretzel croissant and drizzled with a smooth hollandaise sauce. This decadent and delicious dish makes the perfect lazy Sunday brunch.

60 g/4 tablespoons butter
4 slices of bacon
2 teaspoons white or rice vinegar
4 eggs
4 pretzel croissants, sliced
butter, for spreading
8 slices of Brie cheese
a dash of Tabasco sauce (optional)
couple of sprigs of flat-leaf parsley, chopped, to garnish
freshly ground black pepper

HOLLANDAISE SAUCE
140 g/1¼ sticks unsalted butter
3 egg yolks
1 tablespoon freshly squeezed lemon juice
½ teaspoon salt

SERVES 4

To make the hollandaise sauce, melt the butter in a small saucepan. Put the egg yolks, lemon juice and salt in a blender and blend on medium to medium-high speed for 25 seconds or until the egg yolks lighten in colour. Change the blender speed to the lowest setting and very slowly, pour in the hot butter and continue to blend. Add more salt and lemon juice to taste. Transfer to a small jug/pitcher.

Melt some butter in a large frying pan/skillet on a low–medium heat, and when the pan is hot, add the bacon, turning it occasionally until warm.

While the bacon is cooking, fill a large saucepan with water and bring to the boil. Add the vinegar and let it come to a boil again. After the water boils, reduce the heat to a simmer.

Next, poach the eggs. The easiest way is to do one egg at a time. Crack the egg into a small bowl and slip it into the barely simmering water. Once the egg begins to solidify, slip in the next egg and so on until you have all 4 cooking. Turn the heat off, cover the pan with a lid and let the eggs sit for 3–4 minutes, depending on how runny you like your eggs. Starting with the first egg you cracked, gently lift the eggs out with a slotted spoon, pat dry with a paper towel and set them down in a bowl or on a plate.

Toast and butter the pretzel croissants. Top with the bacon, 2 slices of Brie and a poached egg. Sprinkle on Tabasco sauce if liked. Pour the hollandaise sauce over the top and garnish with flat-leaf parsley and ground black pepper, to taste.

Ingredients

2 fillets of cod or haddock, skinned and boned
sunflower or vegetable oil, for frying
thickly cut fresh bread, to serve
butter, for spreading

Beer Batter
200 g/1½ cups plain/all-purpose flour
2 teaspoons sea salt
2 x 330-ml/11-fl. oz. bottles of lager

Tartare Sauce
225 g/1 cup mayonnaise
80 g/½ cup pickles/gherkins
1 teaspoon capers, chopped
2 teaspoons Dijon mustard
2 teaspoons chopped shallots
2 tablespoons chopped spring onions/scallions
2 teaspoons freshly squeezed lemon juice
Tabasco sauce, to taste
sea salt and freshly ground black pepper

To Serve
a handful of cos/romaine lettuce leaves, cut into strips
French fries or sweet potato fries (optional)

Serves 2

Posh fish finger sandwich & homemade tartare sauce

The posh fish finger sandwich makes a fantastic brunch dish. Lager is often used in the batter for a richer flavour. Homemade tartare sauce and French fries finish the meal.

Prepare your fish for battering. Slice the fish into at least six finger-size strips.

For the beer batter, whisk the flour, salt and lager in a bowl until combined. Fill a large frying pan/skillet with about 2.5 cm/ 1 inch of oil over a high heat, but don't leave this unattended. When the oil is bubbling steadily, it's ready to go.

Dip the fish fingers in the batter, remove any excess and then lower carefully into the oil using tongs if necessary. Fry for about 4 minutes on each side over a moderate heat until golden and crispy.

Remove the fish fingers carefully from the oil and drain well on paper towels. Season with sea salt.

Mix all the ingredients for the tartare sauce together in a mixing bowl. Lay one slice of bread down and butter it, then spread a couple of tablespoons of tartare sauce on top. Add 3 fish fingers, then a few strips of lettuce and top with the second slice of bread. Serve with fries, if you like.

Steak & egg breakfast tacos

It's usually the breakfast burrito that steals the show, but these steak and egg breakfast tacos are nothing to scoff at. Fried eggs, steak and ketchup keep this dish simple and hearty.

2 beef steaks
1–2 teaspoons olive oil,
   to season the steaks
8 eggs
8 small corn tortillas/tacos
vegetable oil, for shallow frying
tomato ketchup, for topping
salt and freshly ground
   black pepper

SERVES 4

Preheat the oven to 200°C (400°F) Gas 6 and heat a cast-iron skillet (or other heavy-bottomed and oven-safe pan) over a medium heat.

Season the steaks with salt and pepper, using your fingers to rub the seasoning and about 1 teaspoon of olive oil into both sides of each steak. Add the steaks to the preheated pan and cook for 1–2 minutes on each side before sliding the pan into the preheated oven. Cook the steaks for a further 2–3 minutes for medium to medium–well done. Remove the pan from the oven and let the steaks rest for 2 minutes before slicing them into thin strips.

While the steaks rest, fry the eggs. Set a small non-stick frying pan/skillet over a medium heat and add a little vegetable oil. Break in 1 egg. Season with a little salt and fry until the white is set. Remove to a warm plate and repeat with the remaining eggs.

If you can double-task, heat the tortillas, either by holding them directly over a gas flame with metal tongs, or in a cast-iron frying pan/skillet set over high heat. You want them to be puffed and a little blistered.

Place a fried egg on top of each tortilla and place the sliced steak on top of the egg. Top with tomato ketchup and serve immediately.

250 g/2 cups firm mozzarella, grated
60–90 g/2–3 cups fresh baby spinach leaves, destalked
400g/14-oz. can quartered artichoke hearts, drained and halved
1 large ripe tomato, cut into large chunks
60 g/½ cup small balls or sliced rounds of soft white goat's cheese
a large handful of fresh basil leaves
chilli flakes/hot red pepper flakes, to taste (optional)

SIMPLE TOMATO SAUCE
400-g/14-oz. jar of tomato passata/strained tomatoes
1½ teaspoons crushed garlic
1 tablespoon dried oregano
1 teaspoon ground paprika
salt and freshly ground black pepper

PIZZA BASE
7 g/¼ oz. packet active dry yeast
1 teaspoon white sugar
250 ml/1 cup warm water (45°C/110°F)
340 g/2½ cups strong white/ bread flour
2 tablespoons olive oil
1 teaspoon salt
polenta/cornmeal, for dusting

a pizza pan, lightly greased, or a pizza peel or stone

SERVES 2

Spinach, artichoke & goat's cheese pizza

This pizza has a mixture of green vegetables and mild creamy goat's cheese that make it a delicious and masterful way of enjoying pizza. It's both packed with flavour yet light, fresh and nutritious. Virtuous comfort food – what's not to like?

To make the simple tomato sauce, heat the passata/strained tomatoes in a small saucepan with the other sauce ingredients. Bring to the boil, reduce the heat and let simmer for 5 minutes. Season to taste with salt and pepper, remove from the heat and set aside.

Preheat the oven to 230°C (450°F) Gas 8.

For the pizza base, in a medium bowl, dissolve the yeast and sugar in the warm water. Let stand until creamy, about 10 minutes. Stir in the flour, oil and salt. Beat until smooth, then let rest for 5 minutes. Turn the dough out onto a lightly floured surface and pat or roll into a round of about 30 cm/12 inches. Transfer the crust to the lightly greased pizza pan or onto a baker's peel dusted with polenta/cornmeal.

Spread 125 ml (½ cup) of tomato sauce on the crust (any leftover sauce can be stored in the fridge for a few days). Sprinkle half of the mozzarella over the tomato sauce. Scatter spinach leaves evenly over the crust, then top with the artichokes and tomato slices. Sprinkle the remaining mozzarella cheese on top (the cheese will hold it together).

Arrange small balls/slices of goat's cheese over the top and add some torn fresh basil leaves to the top of the pizza (reserve a few leaves to garnish).

Bake in the preheated oven for 15–20 minutes, or until golden brown. Let the baked pizza cool for 5 minutes. Sprinkle some chilli flakes/hot red pepper flakes over the top, if using, and some more fresh basil, then slice and serve immediately.

Triple meat & Cheddar breakfast quiche

This is the ultimate quiche for meat-lovers! It is filled with sausage, bacon and ham — the trinity of breakfast meats — and mixed with eggs and milk for a fluffy and hearty (but not too heavy) meal. The flaky pie crust gives this dish amazing texture. It's equally delicious served warm or cold.

FILLING
4 slices of streaky/fatty bacon
2 pork sausages
6 eggs, well beaten
125 ml/½ cup full-fat/whole milk
¼ teaspoon salt
a pinch of freshly ground
   black pepper
60 g/½ cup chopped lean ham
2 large spring onions/
   scallions, sliced
90 g/1 cup grated/shredded
   Cheddar cheese

PIE CRUST DOUGH
130 g/1 cup plain/
   all-purpose flour
½ teaspoon salt
60 ml/¼ cup olive oil
60 ml/¼ cup ice-cold water

*a 23-cm/9-inch tart pan,
   lightly greased*

MAKES 1 QUICHE

To make the pie crust, put the flour and salt in a mixing bowl and stir with a fork to combine. Beat the oil and water together with a small whisk or fork until emulsified. Pour the water and oil mixture into the flour and mix with a fork. Roll the dough into a ball, wrap in clingfilm/plastic wrap and refrigerate for at least 30 minutes before using.

To prepare the quiche filling, cook the bacon in a dry frying pan/skillet until crisp. Remove from the pan and set aside. Remove the skins from the sausages and add the sausage meat to the pan. Cook it over medium–high heat, breaking it up with a wooden spoon, until cooked through. Crumble the cooked bacon and set the crumbled bacon and sausage aside.

Preheat the oven to 220°C (425°F) Gas 7. Roll out the chilled pastry/pie dough and press it into the prepared tart pan. Prick the base with a fork and bake in the preheated oven for about 10 minutes, until lightly browned.

In a large bowl, whisk together the eggs, milk, salt and pepper. Arrange the cooked bacon, sausagemeat and ham in the part-baked pie crust and evenly sprinkle the spring onions/scallions and cheese over the top. Carefully pour the egg mixture on top, taking care not to overfill the pie crust.

Bake the quiche in the preheated oven for about 20–25 minutes, until the filling is set in the centre and a cocktail stick/toothpick comes out clean. Allow to cool slightly before serving.

Tomato bacon gratin

Juicy, naturally sweet tomatoes and salty bacon are one of those great flavour combinations. Serve this simple-to-make dish for breakfast or brunch with thick slices of fresh bread on the side.

1 tablespoon olive oil
2 slices of bacon, finely chopped
1 shallot, peeled and
  finely chopped
25 g/½ cup fresh breadcrumbs
a pinch of dried oregano
4 tomatoes
10 g/2½ tablespoons grated/
  shredded Parmesan cheese
salt and freshly ground
  black pepper

*a shallow ovenproof
  casserole dish, greased*

SERVES 4

Preheat the oven to 200°C (400°F) Gas 6.

Heat the oil in a small frying pan/skillet set over a medium heat. Add the bacon and shallot and fry for 2–3 minutes, stirring often, until the shallot has softened and the bacon is cooked. Remove from the heat and stir in the breadcrumbs and oregano.

Slice the tomatoes into 1-cm/⅜-inch thick slices. Arrange in the prepared casserole dish, overlapping slightly. Season with a little salt and pepper, bearing in mind the saltiness of the bacon.

Spread the bacon mixture evenly over the tomato slices, then sprinkle over the Parmesan. Bake in the preheated oven for 20 minutes and serve hot from the oven.

Salads & Sides

Roasted beetroot, red quinoa, strawberry & basil salad

Sun-blush tomato, orange & burrata salad

Heirloom tomato & smoked mackerel salad

Warm chickpea & spinach salad

Sweet potato, pea & mint fritters

Avocado whip

Sourdough toast toppings

Buttered mushrooms

Scorched ricotta with herbs & honey

Roasted beetroot, red quinoa, strawberry & basil salad

Made sweeter with a scattering of strawberries, this light brunch can be enjoyed in the mid- to late summer months, when both strawberries and beetroot/beets are in season.

3 medium raw mixed purple
   and golden beetroot/beets
   (including the tops)
2 tablespoons honey
2 tablespoons balsamic vinegar
2 tablespoons olive oil
3 sprigs of fresh thyme
170 g/1 cup red quinoa
150 g/1½ cups fresh strawberries,
   trimmed and sliced
2 small handfuls of fresh
   basil leaves
100 g/½ cup crumbled
   goat's cheese
edible flowers, to garnish
   (optional)

DRESSING
3 tablespoons balsamic vinegar
3 tablespoons olive oil
1 garlic clove, finely chopped
1 tablespoon strawberry
   jam/jelly
1 tablespoon wholegrain
   mustard
a pinch each of salt and freshly
   ground black pepper

a baking sheet lined with foil

SERVES 4–6

Preheat the oven to 190°C (375°F) Gas 5.

Start by roasting the beetroot/beets. Cut off the tops and bottoms, reserving the tops. Give the beetroot/beets a good scrub and cut into quarters. Spread out on the prepared baking sheet, drizzle over 2 tablespoons of water, the honey, balsamic vinegar and olive oil, and scatter over the thyme. Fold up the sides of the foil so that the beetroot/beets are covered. Pop into the preheated oven and roast for 50 minutes. They should now be soft all the way through if you poke them with a knife. Remove from the oven and leave to cool. Once cooled slightly, peel off the outer skins.

Wash the beetroot/beet tops thoroughly to get rid of any grit and chop the leaves finely. You will need about 2 handfuls of chopped leaves.

To cook the quinoa, just put it in a saucepan with 500 ml/ 2 cups of water, bring to the boil, then turn the heat down to a gentle simmer. Put a lid on the pan and leave to cook for 10–12 minutes, or until the water has been absorbed. Leave to cool.

To make the dressing, simply add all the ingredients to a clean jar, screw on the lid and shake well to mix. Alternatively, whisk/ beat everything together in a small bowl until well combined.

Once everything has cooled down, you can assemble the salad. Put the quinoa, beetroot/beets, strawberries, beetroot/ beet tops and dressing into a large mixing bowl and toss together. Sprinkle with basil and goat's cheese. You can serve this salad with some edible flowers sprinkled on top – it makes a really beautiful centrepiece for a summer brunch.

Sun-blush tomato, orange & burrata salad

Gloriously simple to put together, this bright and colourful dish offers a Mediterranean-inspired combination of colours, textures and flavours.

2 large oranges
24 sun-blush/semi-dried
   cherry tomato halves
   (see below recipe)
2 burrata cheeses (or good-
   quality fresh mozzarella
   cheese)

**Sun-blush/Semi-dried
   Tomatoes**
450 g/1 lb. ripe but firm
   tomatoes, halved
1 teaspoon olive oil
a pinch of salt
a pinch of sugar
a pinch of dried oregano
   or basil

To Serve
extra virgin olive oil
freshly ground black pepper
a handful of fresh basil leaves

Serves 4

To make the sun-blush/semi-dried tomatoes, preheat the oven to 110°C (225°F) Gas ¼. Place the tomatoes skin side-down on a baking sheet. Sprinkle evenly with the oil, salt, sugar and dried oregano or basil. Bake in the preheated oven for around 3½ hours, until they have softened and partly dried out. Allow the tomatoes to cool, then store in an airtight container in the fridge, and use within a few days.

Peel the oranges, making sure to trim off all the white pith, and cut into even, thick slices.

Place the orange slices on a large serving dish, then scatter over the sun-blush/semi-dried tomato halves. Tear the burrata cheeses into chunks and layer on top of the orange slices.

Drizzle with extra virgin olive oil and season with pepper. Garnish with basil leaves and serve at once.

Heirloom tomato & smoked mackerel salad

100 g/2 cups rocket/arugula
3 heirloom tomatoes, sliced
freshly squeezed juice
 of ½ lemon
a pinch of salt
1 tablespoon olive oil
2 smoked mackerel fillets
 (peppered fillets work well)

Caramelized Onions
2 tablespoons olive oil
1 large red onion, sliced
1 tablespoon red wine vinegar

Greek Yogurt Dressing
115 g/½ cup Greek yogurt
1½ tablespoons freshly
 chopped mint
1 tablespoon freshly chopped
 flat-leaf parsley
1 garlic clove, finely chopped
¼ cucumber, finely chopped
a pinch each of salt and freshly
 ground black pepper
1 teaspoon honey
½ teaspoon lemon zest

Serves 2

This delicious saltiness of this oily fish makes it the perfect partner for the heirloom tomatoes and caramelized onions. This is perfect for a summertime brunch, when tomatoes are in season and a lighter dish fits the bill.

Start by making the caramelized onions. Heat the oil in a frying pan/skillet over a low heat, add the onion and cook slowly for 10 minutes, stirring every now and then. Once soft and beginning to caramelize, add the vinegar and cook for a further minute. Take off the heat.

Whisk/beat all the ingredients for the Greek yogurt dressing together in a small bowl and set aside.

Put the rocket/arugula and tomatoes into a large mixing bowl with the lemon juice, salt and olive oil. Toss to coat everything in oil, then arrange on serving plates.

Break the mackerel up using your hands – this way you can feel for bones and discard any. Arrange the mackerel on top of the salad. Top with the caramelized onions and spoon over the dressing. Serve immediately.

Warm chickpea & spinach salad

The warmth of the lightly spiced chickpeas combines so well with fresh tastes of lemon, parsley, red onion and spinach, making this a superb brunchtime side dish.

2 tablespoons olive oil
1 garlic clove, crushed
¼ teaspoon ground cumin
¼ teaspoon dried thyme or
    ½ teaspoon fresh thyme
    leaves
a 400-g/14-oz. can of chickpeas,
    drained
100 g/2 cups baby spinach
3 tablespoons freshly chopped
    flat-leaf parsley
grated zest of 1 lemon
2 tablespoons finely chopped
    red onion

Tahini Dressing
2 tablespoons tahini
2 tablespoons olive oil
freshly squeezed juice of 1 lemon
a pinch each of salt and freshly
    ground black pepper

Serves 2–4

First, make the tahini dressing. Simply stir all the ingredients together in a bowl with 1 tablespoon of water. (It helps sometimes to give the tahini a really good stir in the pot so it becomes a bit runny.)

Heat the olive oil in a large frying pan/skillet over a low–medium heat. Add the garlic, cumin and thyme, and cook together for 30 seconds. Add the chickpeas, reduce the heat to low and continue to cook for 5 minutes. Add 2 tablespoons of water and leave to cook for another 3 minutes. You can squash the chickpeas a little while they are cooking, if you like.

Lastly, stir in the spinach, chopped parsley, lemon zest and red onion.

Tip into a serving dish, pour the tahini dressing over the top and toss together.

Sweet potato, pea & mint fritters

Not only can these fritters be served at brunch, but they're also brilliant as a side dish to meat, poultry or fish for dinner, or in a wrap with salad for lunch.

2 eggs
1 sweet potato, peeled, grated and squeezed of moisture
80 g/½ cup petit pois
2 spring onions/scallions, chopped
3 tablespoons plain/all-purpose flour
4 sprigs of fresh mint, leaves removed and chopped
1 tablespoon olive oil
salt and freshly ground black pepper
coconut oil, for frying

Makes 10–12 Fritters

Whisk the eggs well in a small bowl. Combine with the sweet potato, peas, spring onions/scallions, flour, mint, olive oil and salt and pepper, mixing well.

In a large pan, melt the coconut oil over a medium heat. Spoon in the potato mixture, 1 generous tablespoon at a time, and pat down into a flat patty with a spatula. Cook for 4 minutes on each side until golden and crispy. Remove from the pan with a spatula, drain on paper towels and serve with the Avocado Whip (see right).

Avocado whip

This avocado whip has a smoothness to it and works nicely as a side dip for brunchtime salads, savoury bakes or waffles. For a creamier and fluffier consistency, use a Nutribullet-type blender — it's worth it. However, if you are in the chunky-avo-is-best brigade, coarsely chop all the ingredients instead.

2 avocados, peeled and stoned/pitted
a handful of spinach
a handful of parsley
juice of 1 lemon
30 ml/2 tablespoons olive oil
salt and freshly ground black pepper

Serves 6

In a food processor, blitz the avocado, spinach, parsley, lemon juice, olive oil and salt and pepper into a smooth, light and fluffy paste. Transfer to a bowl to serve as a side dip to the fritters on the left or other savoury brunch dishes in this book.

Sourdough toast toppings

A brown rye sourdough works well with both sweet or savoury toppings. Buy a good sourdough loaf from your local bakery and serve thick toasted slices with the following toppings.

Whipped honey vanilla butter

150 g/1¼ sticks salted butter, softened
1 teaspoon vanilla paste
2 tablespoons runny honey
bee pollen, to sprinkle

Place the softened butter, vanilla paste and honey in a bowl. Using a hand-held mixer, whisk the ingredients together until light and fluffy. Serve sprinkled with bee pollen.

Crushed berries & goat's curd

500 g/3 cups frozen berries
2 tablespoons sugar
1 teaspoon vanilla paste
100 g/¾ cup goat's curd, to serve

Place the berries, sugar and vanilla paste in a saucepan and heat gently, crushing the berries with a fork. Do not overcook as you want to retain some texture. Serve with the goat's curd.

Tahini maple spread

100 g/½ cup tahini
2 tablespoons maple syrup
1–2 tablespoons warm water
sesame seeds, to sprinkle

Place the tahini and maple syrup in a bowl and mix well. Add the warm water to loosen the spread. Sprinkle with sesame seeds and serve.

Avocado & salmon

2–3 avocados, peeled, stoned/ pitted and sliced
200 g/1 cup smoked salmon
a handful of large capers
lemon, sliced, to serve

Assemble the ingredients on a large platter and allow your guests to top their own toast with the avocados, salmon, capers and a slice of lemon.

Broad bean, courgette & goat's curd

1 tablespoon olive oil
1 courgette/zucchini, thinly sliced into half moons
2 spring onions/scallions, sliced
150 g/1¼ cups frozen broad/ fava beans, defrosted and skins removed
a handful of parsley, finely chopped
a handful of chives, finely snipped
juice of ½ lemon
grated zest of 1 lemon
100 g/¾ cup goat's curd, to serve
sea salt and freshly ground black pepper

Heat the oil in a frying pan/ skillet. Add the courgette/ zucchini, spring onions/ scallions and broad/fava beans. Cook for 10 minutes – they should be just cooked and retain some bite. Place in a bowl and finish with the herbs, lemon juice and zest, goat's curd and salt and pepper.

Buttered mushrooms

The creaminess of the mushrooms combines so well with the sharp and tangy lemony sauce. Serve them piled on top of toasted baguettes or alongside the Sweet Potato, Spinach and Red Onion Frittata (see photo on page 5 and recipe on page 65).

400 g/5 cups mixed mushrooms
60 g/½ stick unsalted butter
1 banana shallot or small onion, thinly sliced
2 garlic cloves, thinly sliced
grated zest of 1 lemon
juice of ½ lemon
½ bunch of flat-leaf parsley, roughly chopped (optional)
2–3 sprigs of fresh lemon thyme
salt and freshly ground black pepper
buttered, toasted baguettes and extra lemon wedges, to serve

SERVES 4 AS A SIDE

Brush the mushrooms clean, halve the larger ones and set aside.

Heat the butter in a large frying pan/skillet over a medium-high heat until foaming. Add the shallot and garlic and cook for about 4–5 minutes, until soft. Add the mushrooms and cook, stirring, for another 4–5 minutes, until just tender. Add the lemon zest and juice and herbs and season to taste.

Serve with buttered toasted baguettes and lemon wedges.

Scorched ricotta with herbs & honey

With only a handful of ingredients, this dish is so simple, but so impressive – the best things always are.

225 g/1 cup ricotta cheese
4 sprigs of fresh thyme
salt and freshly ground black pepper
30 ml/2 tablespoons runny honey

SERVES 6

Preheat the oven to 180°C (350°F) Gas 4. Preheat the grill/broiler to a high temperature.

Place the ricotta in an ovenproof dish, sprinkle with thyme, salt and pepper and drizzle the runny honey over. Place the dish under the grill/broiler and allow the ricotta to scorch and the honey to caramelize – this should take 5–10 minutes, depending how hot the grill/broiler is, so keep an eye on it.

Once you have achieved a scorched colour, move the dish to the preheated oven and bake for a further 10 minutes. Serve warm.

Pastries & Breakfast Bakes

Butterscotch-bacon brittle cinnamon rolls

Beignets

Carrot cake scones

Spelt, banana & chocolate muffins

Quick cornbread

Marmite (yeast extract) cake

Blush tomato & feta muffins

Green garlic muffins

Butterscotch-bacon brittle cinnamon rolls

These maple-bacon cinnamon rolls are very more-ish and delicious served alongside a Coffee Granita (see page 136).

BUTTERSCOTCH-BACON BRITTLE
450 g/1 lb. cooked bacon,
  finely chopped
115 g/1 stick butter
100 g/½ cup caster/
  granulated sugar
225 g/1 cup butterscotch chips

CINNAMON ROLLS
7-g/¼-oz. packet active
  dried yeast
250 ml/1 cup warm milk
100 g/½ cup white sugar
75 g/5 tablespoons butter
1 teaspoon salt
2 eggs
500 g/4 cups plain/
  all-purpose flour

FILLING
180 g/1 cup packed brown sugar
2½ tablespoons ground
  cinnamon
75 g/5 tablespoons soft butter

ICING
115 g/1 stick butter
200 g/1½ cups icing/
  confectioners' sugar
75 g/¼ cup cream cheese
½ teaspoon vanilla extract
a pinch of salt

*a baking sheet lined with
  greased baking parchment*
a large baking pan, lightly greased

MAKES 6–8 ROLLS

Preheat the oven to 200°C (400°F) Gas 6.

For the butterscotch-bacon brittle, spread the bacon on the lined baking sheet. In a medium saucepan, bring the butter and sugar to a boil, stirring and watching constantly as soon as you see the sugar melting. Boil for about 3 minutes, then carefully pour the toffee mixture evenly over the bacon. Bake in the preheated oven for about 4–5 minutes. Remove from the oven and while the toffee is still really hot, sprinkle the butterscotch chips over the top so they melt onto the toffee. Let cool completely before breaking the bacon into pieces. Set aside.

To make the cinnamon rolls, in a large bowl dissolve the yeast in the warm milk. Add the sugar, butter, salt, eggs and flour, and mix well to combine. Turn the dough out onto a lightly floured surface and knead for 5–10 minutes. Bring it together into a large ball, then place in a bowl, cover and let rise in a warm place for about 1 hour or until the dough has doubled in size.

Roll the dough out on a lightly floured surface, until it is approximately 54 x 40 cm/21 x 16 inches and 1 cm/⅓ inch thick.

Preheat the oven to 200°C (400°F) Gas 6.

To make filling, combine the brown sugar and cinnamon in a bowl. Add the butterscotch-bacon brittle. Spread the softened butter over the surface of the dough, then sprinkle the filling mixture evenly over the surface. Working carefully, from the long edge, roll the dough down to the bottom edge. Cut the dough into 4.5-cm/1¾-inch slices.

Place the slices in the prepared baking pan and bake in the preheated oven for 10–12 minutes or until light golden brown. Let cool in the pan.

Combine all the icing ingredients in a large bowl and beat on high speed with an electric mixer until thoroughly combined. Spread the cooled rolls generously with the icing and serve.

Beignets

These New Orleans pillows of heaven are as good as it gets when it comes to doughnuts. Serve with chicory coffee, dip in butter or sugar, or just eat plain.

2¼ teaspoons active dry yeast
375 ml/1½ cups warm water (about 45°C/110°F)
100 g/½ cup caster/granulated sugar
1 teaspoon salt
2 eggs
250 g/1 cup evaporated milk
900 g/7 cups plain/all-purpose flour
60 g/¼ cup shortening
1 litre/4 cups vegetable oil, for deep-frying
35 g/¼ cup icing/confectioners' sugar

MAKES 12 BEIGNETS

In a large bowl, dissolve yeast in the warm water. Add the sugar, salt, eggs and evaporated milk and blend well.

Mix in 500 g/4 cups of the flour and beat until smooth. Add the shortening and then the remaining flour. Cover and chill for up to 24 hours.

Roll out the dough to 3 mm/⅛ inch thick. Cut into 6-cm/2½-inch squares.

Heat the oil for deep-frying to 180°C (360°F).

Fry the beignets in the hot oil in batches until they rise to the surface. (If they do not pop up, the oil is not hot enough.) Remove with a slotted spoon and drain on paper towels.

Shake icing/confectioners' sugar on the hot beignets and serve warm.

Carrot cake scones

260 g/2 cups plain/
   all-purpose flour
1 tablespoon baking powder
50 g/¼ cup soft light brown
   sugar
1 teaspoon salt
1 teaspoon ground cinnamon
¼ teaspoon ground or grated
   nutmeg
¼ teaspoon ground ginger
a pinch of ground cardamom
a pinch of ground all-spice
a pinch of ground cloves
115 g/1 stick unsalted butter,
   cold and cubed
135 g/1 cup grated/shredded
   carrots
70 g/½ cup raisins
180 ml/¾ cup double/heavy
   cream, plus 60 ml/¼ cup
   for brushing

CREAM CHEESE GLAZE
60g/4 tablespoons unsalted
   butter, softened
55 g/¼ cup cream cheese,
   softened
280 g/2 cups icing/
   confectioners' sugar
a pinch of salt
1 teaspoon vanilla extract
1–4 teaspoons milk
50 g/½ cup pecan pieces

a 10-cm/4-inch round
   cookie cutter
a baking sheet lined with
   baking parchment

MAKES 12 SCONES

Carrot cake scones are a great way to get in a dose of carrot cake without the guilt of indulging in a piece of cake for breakfast, although these scones are just as good. They are soft, crisp and spicy. Glaze them or leave them plain, and spread with cream cheese while they are still warm from the oven.

Preheat the oven to 175°C (350°F) Gas 4.

In a large bowl, combine the flour, baking powder, brown sugar, salt and spices. Add the cold diced butter and, using your fingertips, rub the butter into the flour mixture until it resembles coarse crumbs the size of peas. Stir in the carrots and raisins. Pour in the 180 ml/¾ cup double/heavy cream and fold with a rubber spatula until the dough comes together.

Turn out onto a lightly floured work surface and knead a few times. Roll out into a large circle about 2 cm/¾ inch thick. Using the cutter, stamp out scones and place them on the prepared baking sheet. Gather the scraps and gently reroll. Cut out once again. Brush the scones with the extra cream.

Bake in the preheated oven for 20 minutes or until golden brown. Remove from the oven and transfer to a wire rack to cool completely.

To make the cream cheese glaze, mix together all of the ingredients, except the pecans, in a large bowl. Add as much milk as needed to get a pourable consistency, but not too thin. Transfer to a piping/pastry bag with a fine nozzle/tip, and drizzle the glaze over the cooled scones. Sprinkle with chopped pecans and allow to set for a few minutes before serving.

Leftovers can be stored at room temperature, well wrapped, for up to 2 days or in the fridge for up to 4 days. They can also be frozen.

Spelt, banana & chocolate muffins

These are earthy, sweet and chocolatey, but lighter than a traditional stodgy muffin. They can be made ahead and frozen, and also make the perfect afternoon treat if they are not all eaten at brunch.

1 teaspoon baking powder
1 teaspoon bicarbonate of/
  baking soda
a pinch of salt
150 g/1¼ sticks unsalted butter,
  softened
250 g/1¼ cups soft brown sugar
2 eggs, lightly beaten
2 very ripe bananas,
  mashed with a fork
100 g/½ cup Greek yogurt
230 g/1¾ cups spelt flour
60 g/½ cup dark chocolate chips
cocoa powder, to serve

*a 12-hole muffin pan
  lined with muffin cases*

MAKES 12 MUFFINS

Preheat the oven to 170°C (325°F) Gas 3.

Place all the ingredients except the spelt flour and chocolate chips in a food processor and pulse until smooth, then add the spelt flour and chocolate chips by hand and gently mix.

Transfer the mixture to the prepared muffin cases and bake in the preheated oven for 25–30 minutes, or until the muffins are firm and golden brown.

Cool in the pan for 10 minutes before turning out onto a wire rack to cool completely. Serve dusted with cocoa powder.

Quick cornbread

Quick and easy, this is a bread that can be made in advance and successfully frozen. Perfect served with both sweet and savoury accompaniments (see pages 122–129).

150 g/1 generous cup
   plain/all-purpose flour
3 teaspoons baking powder
1 teaspoon salt
170 g/1 heaping cup polenta/
   cornmeal
1 teaspoon caster/
   granulated sugar
1 teaspoon smoked paprika
250 ml/1 cup milk
4 sprigs of fresh oregano, leaves
   removed and chopped, plus
   extra to sprinkle over the top
   before cooking
160 g/1 heaping cup canned
   sweetcorn/corn kernels,
   reserving a tablespoon
   to sprinkle over the top
   before cooking
60 ml/¼ cup olive oil
1 egg, lightly whisked
honey, to drizzle

*a 13 x 24-cm/5 x 10-inch loaf pan,
   greased with olive oil and
   lightly dusted with flour*

MAKES 1 LOAF

Preheat the oven to 220°C (425°F) Gas 7.

In a large bowl mix together all the ingredients and pour the mixture into the prepared pan. Sprinkle over the reserved oregano leaves and sweetcorn/corn kernels.

Bake in the preheated oven for 30–35 minutes or until a skewer inserted into the centre comes out clean. Set aside to cool for 5 minutes before turning out onto a wire rack. Serve warm or at room temperature, drizzled with honey.

Marmite (yeast extract) cake

Marmite cake has a rich flavour and is a must-try for all umami enthusiasts. Serve it warm from the oven at brunchtime, sliced into neat slabs.

70 g/½ stick plus
   1 tablespoon butter
170 g/¾ cup plus
   2 tablespoons sugar
1 egg, beaten
160 g/1½ cups plain/
   all-purpose flour
2 teaspoons baking powder
¼ teaspoon salt
250 ml/1 cup whole milk

TOPPING
120 g/1 stick butter
2 teaspoons Marmite/
   yeast extract
60 g/½ cup plus 1 tablespoon
   grated/shredded Cheddar
   cheese

*a 23 x 33-cm/9 x 13-inch
   Pyrex baking dish*

SERVES 10–12

Preheat the oven to 190°C (375°F) Gas 5.

Beat the butter and sugar until light, creamy and smooth. Add the egg and beat well.

Sift the dry ingredients together. Alternate adding the dry ingredients and the milk to the butter mixture. Mix gently until well combined and the batter is smooth. Pour the batter into the baking dish and bake in the preheated oven for 25–30 minutes.

To make the topping, simply melt the butter and mix in the Marmite/yeast extract.

Five minutes before the cake is ready, remove from the oven and prick all over with a fork. Pour over the melted butter and Marmite mixture and sprinkle with the grated/shredded Cheddar cheese.

Return to the oven for the final 5 minutes until the cake is cooked and a skewer inserted into the centre comes out clean, and the cheese has melted and turned slightly golden. This cake is best served warm from the oven.

Blush tomato & feta muffins

Who doesn't love a savoury muffin? These combine the rich, crumbly textures of feta cheese with the sweet, ripened flavour of sun-blush/semi-dried tomatoes (see page 91). Enjoy for breakfast and brunch alongside other savoury accompaniments.

75 g/5 tablespoons butter, melted
2 eggs
140 ml/²/₃ cup whole milk
300 g/2¹/₃ cups self-raising/ rising flour
1 teaspoon baking powder
1 teaspoon salt
2–3 pinches of dried oregano
14 sun-blush/semi-dried tomatoes, chopped
100 g/3¹/₂ oz. feta cheese, diced

a 12-hole muffin pan, lined with 10 muffin cases

MAKES 10 MUFFINS

Preheat the oven to 200°C (400°F) Gas 6.

Whisk or beat together the melted butter, eggs and milk in a large mixing bowl.

In a separate bowl, sift the flour and baking powder together, then stir in the salt and oregano. Pour in the melted butter mixture and quickly and lightly fold into the flour. Stir through the tomatoes and feta.

Divide the mixture evenly between the muffin cases and bake in the preheated oven for 20–25 minutes until risen and golden-brown. Serve the muffins warm from the oven or at room temperature.

Green garlic muffins

These tasty muffins, flecked with grated courgette/zucchini and chopped pistachio nuts, are great for brunch. Serve warm from the oven with butter, cream cheese or your favourite savoury spread.

1 teaspoon olive oil

2 garlic cloves, chopped

225 g/1¾ cups self-raising/self-rising flour

1 teaspoon baking powder

1 teaspoon salt

1 egg

50 g/4 tablespoons plain/natural yogurt

100–125 ml/⅓–½ cup whole milk

150 g/1¾ cups grated/shredded courgettes/zucchini

50 g/½ cup chopped pistachio nuts

50 g/½ cup grated/shredded Cheddar cheese

a 12-hole muffin pan lined with muffin cases

MAKES 12 MUFFINS

Heat the oil in a small frying pan/skillet and gently fry the garlic until golden, stirring and taking care not to burn it. Set aside to cool.

Preheat the oven to 200°C (400°F) Gas 6.

Sift the flour, baking powder and salt into a mixing bowl. In a separate bowl, whisk together the egg, yogurt and 100 ml/⅓ cup milk. Pour the egg mixture over the sifted ingredients and stir together, taking care not to over-mix. If the mixture appears very dry then add the extra milk. Fold in the fried garlic, courgettes/zucchini, pistachios and Cheddar cheese.

Divide the mixture among the muffin cases. Bake in the preheated oven for 20 minutes until risen and golden brown. Serve warm from the oven or allow to cool.

Preserves
& Drinks

Grape jelly · Lemon curd

Lime marmalade · Passion fruit curd

Tomato vanilla jam · Thai tomato jam

Spiced red tomato chutney · Green tomato chutney

Flavoured waters

Pomegranate & mint green tea · Green piña colada smoothie

Green tea granita · Umami bloody Mary

Coffee granita · Espresso Martini

Blueberry coffee · Italian coffee

Pickle-back Martini · The Sergeant Pepper

Grape jelly

Peeling grapes can be a bit tedious, but once you taste this jelly, you'll realize it was worth the effort.

1.35 kg/3 lb. ripe Concord grapes,
  picked off of their stems
600 g/3 cups sugar

sterilized glass jars (see page 4)

MAKES ABOUT 1.25 KG/2¾ LBS.

Preheat the oven to 75°C (150°F) or your lowest gas setting.

Peel the skins off the grapes. Set aside the grape skins; you will be using them later.

Put the pulp in a saucepan and place over a medium heat. Cover and cook for 5 minutes, stirring occasionally. When the grapes have broken down to a mush, remove from the heat.

Set a sieve/strainer over a large bowl. Pour the grape pulp into the sieve/strainer and, using a wooden spoon, push the pulp through the mesh. Discard the seeds. Put the pulp back in the saucepan.

Put the sugar in a baking pan and place in the low oven to warm.

Add the grape skin to the pulp and bring it to a boil, stirring occasionally. Boil for 2 minutes. The mixture will turn dark due to the colour of the grape skins. Gradually add the warm sugar to the pulp, stirring in 250 ml/ 1 cup at a time. Bring back to a rolling boil and cook, stirring constantly. When it thickens, remove from the heat and let cool a little, then pour into sterilized jars.

Lemon curd

Lemon juice, zest, butter and sugar combine to make a sublime curd.

4 egg yolks
100 g/½ cup caster/granulated sugar
finely grated zest of 5–6 lemons
80 ml/⅓ cup freshly squeezed lemon juice
  (from 3–4 lemons)
a pinch of fine salt
90 g/6 tablespoons unsalted butter,
  cut into 6 pieces, at room temperature

MAKES ABOUT 250 G/9 OZ.

Fill a medium saucepan with 2.5–5 cm/ 1–2 inches of water and bring it to a simmer over a high heat. Reduce the heat to low and keep the water at a bare simmer.

Place all the ingredients except the butter in a large heatproof bowl and whisk or beat to combine. Set the bowl over, but not touching, the simmering water. Whisk constantly until the yolks thicken and the mixture forms ribbons when the whisk is lifted, about 7–10 minutes. (Check the water does not boil by periodically removing the bowl from the pan. If it boils, reduce the heat so the eggs do not curdle.) Remove the bowl from the simmering water and whisk in the butter a piece at a time, waiting until each piece is completely melted and incorporated before adding another.

Set a fine-mesh sieve/strainer over a bowl. Strain the curd, pressing on the solids and scraping the curd from the underside of the mesh. Discard the solids left in the strainer. Press clingfilm/plastic wrap directly onto the surface of the curd to prevent a skin forming. Refrigerate until set, at least 3 hours.

Lime marmalade

As easy to make as to eat.

6 small limes
3 unwaxed lemons
2 kg/9 cups granulated white sugar

sterilized glass jars (see page 4)

Makes about 1.3 kg/3 lbs.

Scrub the fruit, cut into quarters and remove the seeds. Fill a large pan with 3 litres/12 cups of water and soak the fruit for 24 hours.

Remove the fruit from the pan (don't discard the water) and cut into small shreds. Return to the water in which it has been soaking, bring to the boil and boil for 1 hour.

Add all the sugar to the pan. Boil again until the juice forms a jelly when tested. To test if the marmalade is ready, place 2 teaspoons of the mixture on a cold saucer. Press the surface of the marmalade with your thumb and if it wrinkles, it is done. Let cool for 10 minutes.

Transfer the marmalade into sterilized jars and seal. Store in a dark, cool place and, for the best taste, leave to set for 1 month.

Passion fruit curd

If you are a fan of lemon curd (see page 122), you will adore this. It is a little more perfumed than its lemony relative and somewhat sweeter. It goes brilliantly on any kind of bread.

150 ml/$\frac{2}{3}$ cup passion fruit pulp
  (from about 6 fruit)
freshly squeezed juice of 1 lemon
3 whole eggs
3 egg yolks
100 g/$\frac{1}{2}$ cup golden caster sugar
100 g/7 tablespoons unsalted butter,
  chilled and cubed

sterilized glass jars (see page 4)

Makes about 500 g/1 lb.

Bring a saucepan of water to the boil.

Take a heatproof bowl that will sit over your pan of boiling water. Sift the passion fruit pulp into the bowl and add the lemon juice, all the eggs and the sugar. Whisk until well mixed, then set the bowl over the top of the pan of boiling water. Reduce the heat to low. Continue to whisk the mixture every 30 seconds, until it thickens, about 10–15 minutes. Turn the heat off and add the cubed butter, whisking it in until the curd thickens.

Remove from the heat and continue to whisk until the mixture has cooled down. Transfer to the sterilized jars. Store in the fridge for up to 2 weeks.

Tomato vanilla jam

Enjoy this ruby-red, sweet preserve on bread, toast or pancakes.

1 kg/2¼ lbs. ripe tomatoes
1 kg/5 cups jam/gelling sugar
freshly squeezed juice of 2 lemons
1 vanilla pod/bean

sterilized glass jars (see page 4)

MAKES ABOUT 1.3 KG/3 LBS.

Scald the tomatoes by pouring boiling water over them in a heatproof bowl. Set aside for 1 minute, then drain and carefully peel off the skin using a sharp knife. Roughly chop and place in a large mixing bowl with their juices, the sugar, lemon juice and vanilla pod/bean. Cover and set aside to macerate for 2 hours.

Meanwhile, place two small side plates in the fridge to use for the setting test.

Transfer the mixture to a large saucepan set over a low heat. Warm, stirring, until the sugar has dissolved. Increase the heat and bring to a rolling boil for 6–10 minutes. To test if the jam is ready, turn the heat off and place a teaspoon of the jam on a cold plate. Leave for 30 seconds, then push the jam with a spoon. If the surface wrinkles, it is ready to bottle. If not, continue simmering and test again in 5 minutes. When the jam is ready, remove from the heat and set aside for 15 minutes.

Skim off any film, then bottle at once in warm, sterilized jars. Seal with new lids and clean screwbands. Keep in a cool, dry place for 4–10 weeks to mature. Once opened, store in the fridge.

Thai tomato jam

Thai lime leaves and lemongrass add a delicious fragrance to this spicy tomato jam, delicious served with bacon or other savoury dishes.

500 g/1 lb. tomatoes
1 fresh red chilli/chile, deseeded
1 garlic clove, peeled and chopped
5-cm/2-inch piece of fresh ginger, peeled and chopped
2 Thai lime leaves, central spines removed and shredded
1 tablespoon Thai fish sauce
100 g/½ cup caster/superfine sugar
50 g/¼ cup dark brown sugar
1 lemongrass stalk, pounded

sterilized glass jars (see page 4)

MAKES ABOUT 440 G/1 LB.

In a food processor, blend together the tomatoes, chilli/chile, garlic, ginger and lime leaves to a purée/paste.

Place the resulting purée/paste in a heavy-based saucepan or pot set over a medium heat. Mix in the fish sauce, both sugars and the pounded lemongrass stalk.

Bring to the boil, stirring all the time. Reduce the heat and simmer uncovered for 1 hour, stirring often to ensure even cooking, until the mixture has thickened and reduced.

Remove and discard the lemongrass stalk and bottle at once in warm, sterilized jars. Seal with new lids and clean screwbands.

Keep in a cool, dry place. Once opened, store in the fridge.

Spiced red tomato chutney

This nicely spicy, rich chutney is a great addition to the brunch table.

3 cardamom pods, lightly crushed
3 whole cloves
1 cinnamon stick
1 kg/2¼ lbs. ripe tomatoes, chopped, juices reserved
700 g/1½ lbs. cooking apples, finely chopped
300 g/10 oz. onions, finely chopped
2 garlic cloves, peeled and chopped
2.5-cm/1-in. piece of fresh ginger, peeled and finely chopped
1 fresh red chilli/chile, finely chopped
200 g/1⅓ cups sultanas/golden raisins
200 g/1 cup soft brown sugar
300 ml/1¼ cups white wine vinegar
2 teaspoons salt

sterilized glass jars (see page 4)

MAKES ABOUT 1.7 KG/3¾ LBS.

Wrap the spices in a small piece of muslin/cheesecloth to form a spice bag. Place with all the other ingredients in a large, nonreactive pan set over a medium heat. Cook, stirring, until the sugar has dissolved. Cover and bring to the boil, then uncover and simmer for 2–3 hours, stirring now and then, until reduced and thickened, with little excess moisture. Test consistency by passing a wooden spoon through the mixture; if it leaves a clean channel, the chutney is ready. Remove the spice bag and bottle at once in warm, sterilized jars. Seal with new lids and clean screwbands. Keep in a cool, dry place for 4–10 weeks to mature. Once opened, store in the fridge.

Green tomato chutney

Unripe 'green' tomatoes, with their firm texture and slightly sour flavour make an excellent tangy chutney.

1 cinnamon stick
4 whole cloves
4 allspice berries
5 black peppercorns
1 kg/2¼ lbs. green tomatoes, chopped
750 g/1¾ lbs. cooking apples, peeled, cored and finely chopped
300 g/10 oz. onions, chopped
150 g/1 cup sultanas/golden raisins
300 g/1½ cups light brown sugar
2 teaspoons salt
350 ml/1½ cups white wine vinegar
½ teaspoon Turkish/Aleppo pepper flakes

sterilized glass jars (see page 4)

MAKES ABOUT 1.4 KG/3 LBS.

Place the cinnamon stick, cloves, allspice and peppercorns in a small muslin/cheescloth bag. Put the spice bag and all the other remaining ingredients in a large, non-reactive pan set over a medium heat.

Bring the mixture to the boil and cook uncovered, stirring now and then, for around 3 hours until it has thickened and reduced, but still has a little excess moisture.

Bottle at once in warm, sterilized jars. Seal with new lids and clean screwbands. Keep in a cool, dry place for 4–10 weeks to mature. Once opened, store in the fridge.

Flavoured waters

Be creative and come up with exciting variations of refreshing flavoured water. These are some favourite combinations to serve alongside any sweet or savoury brunch dish. Add edible flowers to give an ethereal touch.

Lemongrass & cucumber

2 lemongrass stalks, bruised
1 small cucumber, thinly pared
ice
1.5 litres/6 cups water
   (or enough to fill the
   jug/pitcher)

SERVES 6

Mix the lemongrass,
cucumber, ice and water
in a jug/pitcher and serve.

Citrus

¼ grapefruit, thinly sliced
1 lemon, thinly sliced
ice
1.5 litres/6 cups water
   (or enough to fill the
   jug/pitcher)

SERVES 6

Mix the citrus fruits, ice and
water in a jug/pitcher and serve.

Strawberry & basil

5 strawberries, hulled
   and quartered
a bunch of basil
ice
1.5 litres/6 cups water
   (or enough to fill the
   jug/pitcher)

SERVES 6

Mix the strawberries, basil,
ice and water in a jug/pitcher
and serve.

Pomegranate & mint green tea

Green tea and ruby pomegranate jewels work so well together in this tea that will replenish and refresh you.

3 green teabags
2 large sprigs of fresh mint
50 ml/3½ tablespoons pomegranate juice
1 tablespoon pomegranate seeds (optional), plus a few extra to serve in each glass

a 6-cup teapot

SERVES 6

Place the teabags and mint in the teapot. Boil enough water to fill the teapot, let it wait for 3 minutes, then pour into the teapot and allow to infuse for up to 3 minutes.

Remove the teabags from the teapot, add the pomegranate juice and seeds (if using) and serve.

Green piña colada smoothie

Tropical goodness in a glass – or add a shot of Malibu to make it really naughty at brunchtime!

1 pineapple, peeled, cored and roughly chopped
1 banana
freshly squeezed juice of 1 lime
100 ml/scant ½ cup coconut milk
a large handful of spinach
ice cubes
Malibu (optional)

SERVES 6

Blitz all the ingredients together in a blender for a smooth consistency. Add Malibu for a dirty one. Pour into six tall glasses and serve.

Green tea granita

A glass of this refreshing green tea magic is perfect for a summer brunch when the temperature is rising.

4 good-quality green teabags
   or 2 tablespoons loose-leaf green tea
a handful of freshly chopped mint
2.5-cm/1-inch piece of fresh ginger,
   peeled and sliced
a very small pinch of cayenne pepper
freshly squeezed juice of 1 lemon
runny honey, to taste

TO SERVE
sake, chilled (optional)
fresh mint leaves

SERVES 4–6

Put 750 ml/3 cups water in a saucepan over a high heat. When almost boiling, add the tea, mint, ginger and cayenne pepper, then cover and turn off the heat. Leave to sit for 10 minutes to infuse, then strain through a fine sieve/strainer to remove the solids.

Add the lemon juice and honey to taste.

Pour the liquid into a plastic or glass container and place in the freezer for at least 3–4 hours. It is important that every 30 minutes you stir the mixture with a fork to break up the ice crystals.

When ready to serve, if you find the mixture is too slushy, give it a good stir and return to the freezer until more solid, or if you find it is too hard just remove it from the freezer for a few minutes until softened slightly.

Serve in glasses garnished with fresh mint leaves, and with a teaspoon to the side.

Umami bloody Mary

This recipe was inspired by Salvatore Calabrese's Bloody Asparagus recipe in his brilliant book *Cocktails By Flavour*, a must for anyone interested in the intoxicating and the enchanting.

4 fresh asparagus tips
90 ml/6 tablespoons vodka
30 ml/2 tablespoons Clamato juice
   (mix of tomato juice and clam juice)
   or good-quality tomato juice
5 ml/1 teaspoon freshly squeezed lemon juice
6 dashes of Worcestershire sauce
4 dashes of Tabasco
2 pinches of salt
3 twists of freshly ground black pepper

TO GARNISH
a saucer of soy sauce
celery salt, for dipping
2 fresh asparagus spears
1 lemon slice, cut in half

SERVES 2

Muddle the asparagus in the bottom of a cocktail shaker. Add the remaining ingredients and ice and shake.

Dip the rim of 2 highball glasses into the soy sauce and then into the celery salt to create an umami-packed rim. Fill the glasses with ice, then strain the tomato mixture into them. Garnish with a spear of asparagus and a lemon slice.

Coffee granita

A deliciously refreshing treat, this granita provides a sweet coffee hit made for sipping.

270 g/9 tablespoons freshly ground
   espresso beans, plus extra to garnish
5 tablespoons sugar
1.2 litres/5 cups boiling water

SERVES 4

Brew fresh, strong coffee with the water and the ground espresso beans. Transfer the hot liquid to a cake pan or freezerproof shallow bowl. Add sugar to taste, stirring to dissolve. Set aside to cool slightly, then transfer to the freezer and freeze, uncovered, for 1 hour.

Remove from the freezer, gently rake the tines of a fork across the surface of the coffee, breaking up any ice crystals in the middle and around the edges. Return to the freezer for a further 45 minutes, then repeat the process.

Repeat the freezing and raking process twice more until all of the coffee is frozen into flaky ice crystals.

To serve, spoon the granita into sundae bowls or Martini glasses, top with a few coffee beans and serve with a teaspoon.

Espresso Martini

The Espresso Martini is a mix of vodka, flavoured liquor and coffee with a kick – perfect for a decadent brunch!

25 ml/1 fl. oz. freshly made espresso
25 ml/2 fl. oz. vodka
25 ml/2 fl. oz. Tia Maria or other
   coffee-flavoured liqueur
ice
orange zest curls, to garnish

SERVES 1

Pour all the ingredients into a shaker. Fill with ice and shake. Strain into a chilled Martini glass. Wait for the cocktail to 'separate' – a foam will rise to the top and the liquid below become clearer.

Garnish with the orange zest curls and serve immediately.

Blueberry coffee

It might sound like an unlikely combination, but the two flavours go extremely well together. The rich and neutral flavour of a blueberry mixed with the dark flavour of coffee highlight each other well.

a pot of freshly brewed coffee
  (4 servings)
cream, to serve (optional)
blueberry coffee syrup
  (see below recipe)

BLUEBERRY COFFEE SYRUP
250 g/2 cups fresh blueberries
70 g/⅓ cup white sugar

SERVES 4

To make the syrup, put blueberries in a blender with 80 ml/⅓ cup water and blend until smooth to make a purée. Strain to remove the seeds. Transfer the purée to a pan and add the sugar. Place over a medium heat and stir constantly until the sugar is dissolved. Set the syrup aside to cool.

Brew the coffee to your liking. Add the blueberry syrup and cream, if using, to taste and serve immediately.

Italian coffee

In Italy, an 'Italian Coffee' would simply be an espresso. However, it's also a cocktail perfect to serve at brunch as it's a variation of the ever-popular 'Irish' Coffee.

4 teaspoons Amaretto or other
  almond-flavoured liqueur
4 tablespoons Tia Maria or other
  coffee-flavoured liqueur
600 ml/20 fl. oz. freshly brewed coffee
sugar, to taste
175 ml/6 fl. oz. whipping cream

SERVES 4

Carefully pour 1 teaspoon of Amaretto and 1 tablespoon of Tia Maria each into 4 heatproof glasses. Top each glass up with hot coffee and stir. Taste and add sugar if needed (you may not need any at all).

Using the back of a teaspoon (or barspoon if you have one), gently pour the cream over the spoon and onto the surface of the drinks to 'float' it on the top. Serve immediately.

Pickle-back Martini

Pickle juice is not an easy-sell when it comes to cocktails. This drink, however, is the perfect cure for a hangover if you are serving brunch the morning after the night before. It's a play on a popular drink called the Pickle-back, which is a shot chased with pickle juice. It's a wonderful drink, but not for the faint hearted.

500 ml/2 cups gin or rye whiskey,
   as preferred
1 teaspoon dry vermouth
   (only if using gin)
4 tablespoons chilled dill pickle juice
4 dill pickle spears
a dash of hot sauce
cubed ice, for shaking

SERVES 4

Make in two batches. Combine half the liquid ingredients in a shaker filled with ice. Shake for 30 seconds and strain into two chilled Martini glasses. Repeat for the second batch and serve immediately, garnished with a pickle spear.

The Sergeant Pepper

This cocktail is essentially a classic Martini mixed with highlights of black pepper and fresh apple. It's warm with floral notes and has a spicy finish. Named after the famous Beatles song, it's a drink that anyone (fan or not) should try at least once.

2 dessert apples, sliced into cubes
150 ml/5 fl. oz. gin
30 ml/1 fl. oz. black pepper syrup
   (see below recipe)
ice, for shaking and serving

BLACK PEPPER SYRUP
30 g/¼ cup crushed black peppercorns
200 g/1 cup sugar

SERVES 4

First make the black pepper syrup. In a medium saucepan set over medium heat, combine the pepper and sugar with 250 ml/1 cup water. Stir until sugar dissolves, then remove from heat. Let cool (use an ice bath if needed immediately).

Make the cocktail in two batches. Muddle half of the apple in two glasses. Pour half the the gin and black pepper syrup into a shaker. Fill with ice and shake for 20–30 seconds. Strain into the two glasses. Repeat and serve as a Martini or in a tumbler on the rocks (cubed ice), as preferred.

Index

Credits

RECIPE CREDITS

CAROL HILKER
Banana bread
  French toast
Beignets
Blueberry coffee
Buttermilk blini
  pancakes with salmon
  & horseradish cream
Butterscotch-bacon
  brittle cinnamon rolls
Carrot cake scones
Cherry & ricotta blintzes
  with sour cherry soup
Coffee granita
Espresso Martini
Fisherman's Wharf
  Benedict on sourdough
Fried green tomato
  Benedict
Grape jelly
Italian coffee
Lemon curd
Paris-style eggs Benedict
Pickle-back Martini
Pork sausage & leek
  waffle with split pea
  'syrup'
Posh fish finger
  sandwich &
  homemade tartare
  sauce
Pulled pork & Cheddar
  hotcakes
Spinach, artichoke &
  goat's cheese pizza
Steak & egg breakfast
  tacos
The Sergeant Pepper
Triple meat & Cheddar
  breakfast quiche

KATHY KORDALIS
Avocado whip
Blueberry & blackberry
  açaí bowls
Breakfast tart
Buttered mushrooms
Flavoured waters
Gluten-free apple
  pancakes
Grainy porridge
Green piña colada
  smoothie
Pomegranate & mint
  green tea
Quick cornbread
Quinoa granola with
  tropical fruit &
  coconut yogurt
Scorched ricotta with
  herbs & honey
Sourdough toast
  toppings
Spelt, banana &
  chocolate muffins
Sweet potato, pea &
  mint fritters

JENNY LINFORD
Baked mushroom
  & egg ramekins
Blush tomato & feta
  muffins
Green garlic muffins
Green tomato chutney
Mushroom, bacon
  & onion pancakes
Scrambled eggs with
  chanterelles
Spiced red tomato
  chutney
Sun-blush tomato,
  orange & burrata salad
Thai tomato jam
Tomato bacon gratin
Tomato vanilla jam

CAROLINE ARTISS
Heirloom tomato &
  smoked mackerel salad
Roasted beetroot, red
  quinoa, strawberry
  & basil salad
Super berry granola
Sweet potato, spinach
  & red onion frittata
Warm chickpea
  & spinach salad

LAURA SANTTINI
Green tea granita
Maple & bacon pancakes
Marmite (yeast extract)
  cake
Simple baked eggs with
  chorizo cornbread
Umami bloody Mary

ROSA RIGBY
Banana pancakes with
  crispy Parma ham
Overnight seed pots
Smoked salmon big
  breakfast
Spiced sweet potato
  porridge

JANET SAWYER
Apple & blueberry
  muffins
French toast a la vanille
Honey & vanilla granola
Sweet potato pancakes
  with cinnamon
  & vanilla

LIZ FRANKLIN
Baked oat milk porridge
  with pears, almonds
  & date syrup
Roasted apricots with
  goat's curd puddles
  & oat clusters

TONIA GEORGE
Melon & raspberry salad
  in stem ginger syrup
Passion fruit curd

URSULA FERRIGNO
Lime marmalade

JENNY TSCHIESCHE
Orange-baked rhubarb

PHOTOGRAPHY CREDITS

ED ANDERSON
Pages 22, 23, 64, 89, 92,
93, 94

PETER CASSIDY
Front cover, pages 9, 53,
84, 85, 75, 90, 117, 120,
127, 128

MOWIE KAY
Pages 4, 5, 7, 10, 11, 12, 15,
16, 17, 19, 33, 41, 63, 68,
97, 98, 101, 110, 113, 130,
131, 133

WILLIAM LINGWOOD
Page 44

STEVE PAINTER
Pages 3, 8, 20, 24, 27, 28,
29, 34, 45, 54, 55, 77, 86

CON POULOS
Pages 37, 67, 114, 134

WILLIAM REAVELL
Page 56

MATT RUSSELL
Page 102

TOBY SCOTT
Back cover and spine,
  pages 30, 42, 46, 49, 50,
71, 72, 76, 79, 80, 83, 105,
106, 109, 123, 137, 138, 141

KATE WHITAKER
Pages 32, 107

CLARE WINFIELD
Pages 1, 2, 38, 39, 58, 59,
60, 118, 119, 124, 125, 132